T H E
BRIDE'S
Etiquette
GUIDE

ETIQUETTE
MADE EASY

PAMELA A. LACH

CHICAGO
REVIEW
PRESS

Library of Congress Cataloging-in-Publication

Lach, Pamela A., 1954-
  The bride's etiquette guide / Pamela A. Lach.
    p.   cm.
  Includes index.
  ISBN 1-55652-299-1 (alk. paper)
  1. Wedding etiquette.   2. Etiquette for women.   I. Title
BJ2051.L29   1998   98-18501
395.2'2--dc21
    CIP

A variety of names has been used for the purpose of illustration. Any similarity to actual people is purely coincidental.

Published by Chicago Review Press, Incorporated
814 North Franklin Street
Chicago, IL 60610

ISBN 1-55652-299-1

Printed in the United States of America
5 4 3

Chapter 7

It's Not as Easy as It Looks: Who Does What When 51

Paying the Piper: Monetary Responsibilities 52

Birds of a Feather Attend Together: Attendant
Responsibilities 55

Chapter 8

What It's All About: The Wedding Ceremony 59

It's Beginning to Look A Lot Like Marriage 60

Picking Their Perches: Ceremony Seating 63

You Can't Roller-skate in a Buffalo Herd: Processional
and Recessional 66

Chapter 9

Decorating the Troops: Military Weddings 71

Chapter 10

Let the Good Times Roll: The Reception 75

Pre-Party Primer 76

Stand by Your Man and Mom and Dad and . . .
The Receiving Line 78

Planned Seating Is Stress-relieving 78

Speak Easy: Toasts 80

The Final Feast: The Reception Meal 81

You Put Your Left Foot in and Shake it All About:
Dancing 83

Chapter 11

It's All in a Name 85

Words to Merge the Connections: Introductions 86

What a Difference a Name Makes: Titles 88

This book is for every bride who is overwhelmed by all the questions that she must answer; befuddled by the countless decisions that she must make; and frustrated by the contradictory and sometimes self-serving advice that she receives.

That is you, isn't it? You genuinely want to come up with the right answers and make suitable decisions. Yet, you don't have time to wade through a huge book every time a question arises, especially when your life and your wedding plans do not necessarily fit a perfect traditional mold.

You need a bridal etiquette book because you only get married once—well, hopefully. There are traditions, customs, and practices that apply to a wedding celebration that are unfamiliar to you. There is no reason that you should know all of the answers. Planning a wedding has not been part of your daily life until now.

Even the simplest wedding requires you to choose among options, answer questions, and prepare a plan. You need this source at your fingertips to guide you through the tangled network of information.

So how do I know so much about weddings? Over the years, I've written four other wedding-related books. I learned about weddings the hard way: by attending and participating in them. After the many fiascoes that occurred at my own, other people asked me to help them avoid such problems. Then their friends and relatives wanted assistance, too. I wrote down practical and realistic advice for wedding planning, saving money, writing thank-you notes, and surviving the initial years of marriage.

An acquaintance, who didn't know that some of my books were about this topic, was speaking about a recent wedding that we attended. Someone (not me) mentioned that the bride could have used a good etiquette book. The acquaintance responded, "Who cares about etiquette nowadays? Who needs to be told what to do by some stuffy prune wearing white gloves and a flowered hat?"

You can imagine how I loved that comment! Actually, I'm wearing jeans as I write this, and I'm neither prim nor pompous. And I haven't worn white gloves or a flowered hat since I was six years old.

From now on, your wedding planning will be easier in many ways. This book is organized into fifteen chapters. Each chapter discusses a large variety of questions and concerns and suggests traditional answers and solutions. In addition, a glossary explains more than eighty common and confusing terms you may encounter. Chapter fifteen, on do-it-yourself etiquette, helps you to apply the basic etiquette principles to any special situations or unique circumstances that relate to your wedding. And finally, in the back of the book, you will find a helpful index.

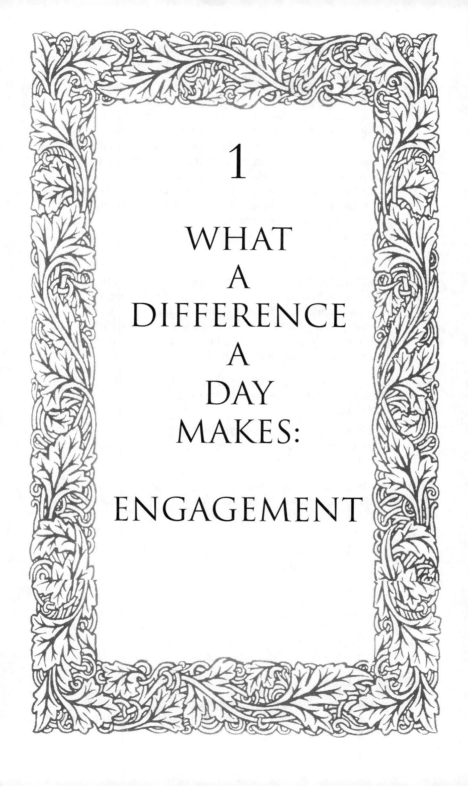

1

WHAT
A
DIFFERENCE
A
DAY
MAKES:

ENGAGEMENT

For Everything, A Reason: Engagement How-to

How long is a traditional engagement?

Most often, the length of the engagement depends on the kind of wedding you want—including which religious denomination you will marry in. Many require a premarital counseling period that can last up to one year. The date you set may be determined by the availability of a certain hall, caterer, or band that you'd like to have. In the peak wedding months of June, July, and August, popular locations might already be reserved two years ahead of time. Your date should be one that fits into your mutual schedules and allows you to have the type of wedding that you desire.

Whom do I tell first?

You should tell both sets of parents, no matter what your age is. If they have never met your fiancé, and you live too far away for a meeting to be practical, at least introduce him by phone. Ideally, your parents and fiancé have already met. If they are unable to meet in person, your parents should then write your fiancé a letter welcoming him to the family.

What if he insists we tell his family first? I want to tell mine first. We can't be in two places at once, unless we each do it alone. Is that the best compromise?

No. Marriage is all about compromise, but you should tell your parents together, unless you are expecting a negative reaction. Traditionally, the bride's parents are told first.

What if I'm closer to someone else? I'm closer to my sister than I am to my mother. Is there any reason I shouldn't tell my sister about the engagement first?

Traditionally, you tell the people who brought you into this world first. Then you tell your siblings, grandparents, aunts, uncles, close friends, and cousins.

When do I tell my children?

Children should be among the first to know. They should definitely know before a former spouse knows. You, the parent, should tell the child, ideally alone, so he or she may raise any fears or concerns out of hearing range of your fiancé.

Should I tell my ex-husband?

It is considerate to personally inform a former spouse of your plans to remarry. He doesn't have to come to the wedding.

Ringing in the Social Graces: Ring Etiquette

Must I have an engagement ring? My fiancé and I can't afford one. My mother insists that without one we aren't really engaged. Is a ring really that important?

Your mother might be confusing an engagement ring with a wedding ring, which is considered necessary in a matrimonial service. Many women marry without ever receiving an engagement ring. It's a nice betrothal gift, an outward sign that the couple intends to marry, but nothing more.

Does it have to be a diamond ring?

No. A diamond is traditional, but you can choose any precious or semiprecious stone that appeals to you.

I want to choose my own ring. My fiancé insists that he's supposed to choose the ring and present it to me. Who's right?

You are. Presenting the ring adds high drama to movies and novels. But in reality, every woman wishes to choose the ring that she will be wearing every day for the rest of her life. Many couples go to the jeweler together. If your fiancé is budget conscious, he might visit the jeweler beforehand and discuss his budget, asking that only rings in a predetermined price range be presented for your inspection.

When may I begin wearing my engagement ring?

As soon as you become engaged and obtain a ring. The man usually presents the ring to the woman privately.

Are there circumstances where I might wear it on my right hand?

Yes. Wearing the engagement ring on the right hand is a tradition of some foreign countries.

When do we purchase our wedding rings?

Rings are usually purchased during the engagement.

Isn't my fiancé supposed to have a ring?

No. Traditionally, the woman receives a ring as part of the marriage ceremony. Customs for men having a ring vary among eras, cultures, and individuals. But, he is just as married with or without the ring.

Should the rings be engraved?

This is a matter of individual choice. If engraving is chosen, it is usually the initials and the wedding date. If you select wider bands, you can include a short, meaningful poetic line.

Let the Word Go Forth:
Announcing the Engagement

How do I officially announce our engagement?

Formally, you announce it through the newspaper and through an engagement party. Informally, you tell friends and family, beginning with those closest to you both.

What if my divorce isn't final yet? My fiancé is pushing me to tell everyone about our engagement now. Shouldn't I wait until the final decree?

Yes, you should wait until your final divorce decree. It's just not right to announce your engagement while you are still married to someone else.

My parents have never met him and now we're engaged. . . .

Break it to your parents gently. Mention your fiancé in phone conversations and letters. Your parents will probably start asking more about him. If you are able to bring your fiancé for a visit, your parents will have a chance to see how wonderful he is. Then announce the happy news.

Why should we announce our engagement in the newspapers?

This is the way you let everyone know about the upcoming happy event. It's the best way to inform your many acquaintances who won't be invited to the various festivities.

When should we notify the newspaper?

Newspaper announcements usually appear three to six months before the wedding date. Some newspapers have explicit rules about the time lapse between the two, so check your newspaper's policy by calling the society or features editor.

Should we send out printed engagement announcements?

No. Printed announcements proclaiming the wedding has taken place are mailed after the wedding. No other announcements are sent.

Would I still announce my engagement if I am a divorcée?

This is generally a personal decision. If your marriage took place just a few years before or if you have several children, you may wish to just inform your friends and family in a more quiet fashion. But there is nothing wrong with announcing the news if you wish to do so.

May I announce my engagement if I am a widow?

The purpose of announcing the marriage is to let every friend and acquaintance know about it. Your remarrying is certainly not an insult to your first husband, so why would announcing the marriage be wrong?

My father is seriously ill. Should we still announce our engagement?

Traditionally, public announcements are avoided during times of death or serious illness in the immediate family. Instead, the news is spread by word of mouth.

In whose name is the announcement presented?

Traditionally, the bride's family announces the engagement. They notify their local newspaper and the local newspaper for the groom's family. Often, the couple lives in an entirely different third location. In this case, the bride or her parents would handle the announcement there.

What about including a photograph with the announcement?

If you wish for a picture to appear, you will probably need a glossy black-and-white photograph of either you or both of you to accompany the form. It is customary to have this photo taken by a professional photographer.

What information is included in the traditional announcement?

Malzahn & Hawkins

Mr. and Mrs. John Robert Malzahn of Tallahassee, Florida, announce the engagement of their daughter Roxanne Marie Malzahn to Justin Michael Hawkins of Orlando, Florida. He is the son of Mr. and Mrs. Albert David Hawkins of Nashville, Tennessee.

A March 2001 wedding is planned.

Miss Malzahn was graduated from Miami State University and is director of operations with Dolphin Product Company.

Mr. Hawkins was graduated from the University of Pennsylvania and is a computer programmer for Dolphin Product Company of Tallahassee.

So few families today are traditional, and one of the biggest points of confusion at weddings is how to word things when variations exist. Here's a run-through of a few possibilities.

Bride's parents are divorced, option 1:

Harvey & Yoder

Mrs. Janice Kay Harvey of Green Bay, Wisconsin, announces the engagement of her daughter Melissa Kay to Joseph Charles Yoder of Milwaukee. Miss Harvey is also the daughter of Mr. Anthony Richard Harvey of Madison. Mr. Yoder is the son of Mr. and Mrs. Kevin Patrick Yoder, also of Madison.

A July 2002 wedding is planned.

Miss Harvey was graduated from the University of Wisconsin and teaches economics at Griffith High School in Milwaukee.

Mr. Yoder was also graduated from the University of Wisconsin. He is a systems analyst for Altoona Programs in Milwaukee.

Bride's parents are divorced, option 2:

Harvey & Yoder

Mrs. Janice Kay Harvey of Green Bay, Wisconsin, and Mr. Anthony Richard Harvey of Madison, announce the engagement of their daughter Melissa Kay to Joseph Charles Yoder of Milwaukee. He is the son of Mr. and Mrs. Kevin Patrick Yoder, also of Madison.

A July 2002 wedding is planned.

Miss Harvey was graduated from the University of Wisconsin and teaches economics at Griffith High School in Milwaukee.

Mr. Yoder was also graduated from the University of Wisconsin. He is a systems analyst for Altoona Programs in Milwaukee.

Bride's mother has remarried:

Sagerman & Wolcott

Mr. and Mrs. Travis J. Colton of Fort Collins, Colorado, announce the engagement of Mrs. Colton's daughter Brenda Joy Sagerman to Phillip Charles Wolcott of Lawton, Oklahoma. Miss Sagerman is also the daughter of Sherman R. Sagerman of Fort Collins. Mr. Wolcott is the son of Mr. and Mrs. Allan K. Wolcott of Lawton.

An August 2003 wedding is planned.
Miss Sagerman was graduated from Syracuse University and is a marketing director for FMB Bank of Lawton.
Mr. Wolcott was graduated from the University of Oklahoma and is program director for WMWI in Lawton.

Bride's father has remarried:

Sagerman & Wolcott

Mr. and Mrs. Travis J. Colton of Fort Collins, Colorado, announce the engagement of Mrs. Colton's daughter Brenda Joy Sagerman to Phillip Charles Wolcott of Lawton, Oklahoma. Miss Sagerman is also the daughter of Mr. and Mrs. Sherman R. Sagerman of Fort Collins. Mr. Wolcott is the son of Mr. and Mrs. Allan K. Wolcott of Lawton.
An August 2003 wedding is planned.
Miss Sagerman was graduated from Syracuse University and is a marketing director for FMB Bank of Lawton.
Mr. Wolcott was graduated from the University of Oklahoma and is program director for WMWI in Lawton.

One of the bride's or groom's parents is deceased

Bride's mother is deceased, father not remarried:

Moore & Fielding

Mr. Joel K. Moore of Hartford, Connecticut, announces the engagement of his daughter Hannah Jane Moore to Richard James Fielding of Stanford. Miss Moore is also the daughter of the late Amelia Burkeston Moore. Mr. Fielding is the son of Mr. and Mrs. Charles C. Fielding, also of Hartford.
A December 2003 wedding is planned.
Miss Moore was graduated from the University of Arizona and is a publicity director for Health Alliance International.
Mr. Fielding was also graduated from the University of Arizona and is curator for the DuPere Historical Museum in Andover.

Bride's mother is deceased, father remarried:

Moore & Fielding

Mr. and Mrs. Joel K. Moore of Hartford, Connecticut, announce the engagement of Mr. Moore's daughter Hannah Jane Moore to Richard James Fielding of Stanford. Miss Moore is also the daughter of the late Amelia Burkeston Moore. Mr. Fielding is the son of Mr. and Mrs. Charles C. Fielding, also of

Hartford.

A December 2003 wedding is planned.

Miss Moore was graduated from the University of Arizona and is a publicity director for Health Alliance International.

Mr. Fielding was also graduated from the University of Arizona and is curator for the DuPere Historical Museum in Andover.

Bride's father is deceased, mother not remarried; fiancé's parents are divorced:

Speer & Collins

Mrs. Warren R. Speer of Richmond, Virginia, announces the engagement of her daughter Sarah Elizabeth Speer to Timothy James Collins of Alma, Michigan. Miss Speer is also the daughter of the late Mr. Warren R. Speer. Mr. Collins is the son of Mr. James T. Collins, also of Alma, and Mrs. Clyde R. Johnson, of Lansing, Michigan.

An April 2004 wedding is planned.

Miss Speer was graduated from Michigan State University and is an audit controller for KVI Systems, Inc.

Mr. Collins was graduated from Central Michigan University and will be locating to the Richmond area.

Bride's father is deceased, mother remarried:

Speer & Collins

Mr. and Mrs. James T. Reed of Richmond, Virginia, announce the engagement of Mrs. Reed's daughter Sarah Elizabeth Speer to Timothy James Collins of Alma, Michigan. Miss Speer is also the daughter of the late Mr. Warren R. Speer. Mr. Collins is the son of Mr. and Mrs. James T. Collins, also of Alma.

An April 2004 wedding is planned.

Miss Speer was graduated from Michigan State University and is an audit controller for KVI Systems, Inc.

Mr. Collins was graduated from Central Michigan University and will be locating to the Richmond area.

One of the groom's parents is deceased:

Harvey & Yoder

Mr. and Mrs. Anthony Richard Harvey of Green Bay, Wisconsin, announce the engagement of their daughter Melissa Kay to Joseph Charles Yoder of Milwaukee. Mr. Yoder is the son of Mrs. Kevin Patrick Yoder of Madison and the late Mr. Kevin

Patrick Yoder.

A July 2002 wedding is planned.

Miss Harvey was graduated from the University of Wisconsin and teaches economics at Griffith High School in Milwaukee.

Mr. Yoder was also graduated from the University of Wisconsin. He is a systems analyst for Altoona Programs in Milwaukee.

Bride is a widow or divorcée:

Bride's parents announce the engagement

Colton & Wolcott

Mr. and Mrs. Travis J. Colton of Fort Collins, Colorado, announce the engagement of their daughter Brenda Joy Sagerman to Phillip Charles Wolcott of Lawton, Oklahoma. Mr. Wolcott is the son of Mr. and Mrs. Allan K. Wolcott of Lawton.

An August 2003 wedding is planned.

Miss Sagerman was graduated from Syracuse University and is a marketing director for FMB Bank of Lawton.

Mr. Wolcott was graduated from the University of Oklahoma and is program director for WMWI in Lawton.

Bride announces the engagement:

Pielow & Everich

The engagement of Ms. Karen Lynn Pielow of Bellingham, Washington, to Mr. Wayne Joseph Everich IV of Seattle has been announced.

An October 2001 wedding has been planned.

Ms. Pielow is a sports announcer for NBC Seattle.

Mr. Everich is director of product development for Microsoft, Inc.

Groom's parents announce the engagement:

Winthrop & Zavacky

The engagement of Natalie Jane Winthrop, daughter of Mr. and Mrs. Ronald L. Winthrop of Mackinac Island, Michigan, to Jeremy Tyler Zavacky, son of Mr. and Mrs. Robert M. Zavacky, Jr., of Valparaiso, Indiana, is announced.

A September 2014 wedding is planned.

Miss Winthrop was graduated from the University of Chicago and is director of Biophysics Laboratories in Northbrook.

Mr. Zavacky was also graduated from the University of Chicago and is owner of eleven sports franchises in the region.

The Best Is Yet to Come:
The Engagement Celebration

What kinds of engagement parties are there?

Engagement parties are usually simple celebrations, along the lines of a cocktail—or cake and punch—gathering. Some prefer a more formal dinner. In truth, you can do whatever you like. There are no hard-and-fast "rules."

When should the engagement party be held?

After you become engaged but before it appears in the newspapers.

Who gives the party?

Traditionally, the bride's family gives the party. However, since so many couples come from different regions, often the groom's family also gives a party as a way to introduce the bride to their family and friends. But, anyone can give the party—some couples even throw one for themselves.

Who should be invited?

Generally, it's a small celebration among close friends and relatives.

Will we receive gifts?

Whether you have a party or not, few people give engagement gifts. They are not expected, although a few people close to you may wish to give you one. They are usually items for your new life together, such as linens, paintings, sculptures, and figurines.

Who makes the official announcement at the party?

Most often, the parents propose a toast to the new couple and welcome the new son (or daughter) into the family. Or, you can make the announcement together.

2

GETTING THERE IS HALF THE FUN:

BEFORE THE WEDDING

What makes a wedding formal? Semiformal? Informal?

Formal:

More than two hundred guests. Traditional plain invitations. Sit-down or semibuffet catered dinner. Up to ten bridesmaids. Bride in long white gown with train. Groom in a cutaway or tailcoat. Ceremony and reception in large, splendid, well-decorated surroundings.

Semiformal:

Between seventy-five and two hundred guests. Less traditional invitations. Dinner is buffet, or hors d'oeuvres and sandwiches. No more than six bridesmaids. Bride in long gown, anywhere from tea-length to floor-length. Groom in tuxedo. Ceremony and reception in less opulent surroundings.

Informal:

Fewer than seventy-five guests. Invitations may be handwritten, computer-generated, or telephoned. Dinner in restaurant or made by friends and relatives; or perhaps just hors d'oeuvres, sandwiches, or cake and punch. Honor attendant and perhaps one bridesmaid. Bride in cocktail-length dress, suit, or very simple long gown. Groom in suit or sports jacket. Ceremony and reception in simple surroundings.

What if my parents want us to elope?

Is it your parents' wedding day? No. They've had their day and made their choices. Perhaps they had an expensive wedding and feel that the cost was not worth the enjoyment. Perhaps they had a very small wedding and do not know what they missed. This is your day, and after politely listening to other people's suggestions, the two of you should select the celebration style that will make you the happiest.

What do I do and when do I do it?

Here's a helpful timetable:

You're engaged!

- ❦ Choose your engagement ring.
- ❦ Ask people to be your attendants and to join your wedding party.
- ❦ Begin to prepare the guest list and ask the groom to do the same.

- 🍂 Compile information about service providers.
- 🍂 Reserve the reception site.
- 🍂 Select the location for the ceremony.
- 🍂 Set a wedding date and time.

The wedding will be in six months.

- 🍂 Choose your attendants' attire.
- 🍂 Discuss possible honeymoon destinations.
- 🍂 Have your fiancé select the formalwear style for the men.
- 🍂 Order your invitations, announcements, and other stationery.
- 🍂 Select your wedding gown and headpiece.

It's four months until the wedding.

- 🍂 Address the invitations and announcements.
- 🍂 Check the requirements for any medical tests.
- 🍂 Confirm that your fiancé has chosen and ordered his attire.
- 🍂 Discover what regulations apply to obtaining a marriage license.
- 🍂 Make an appointment for any physical exams and medical tests.
- 🍂 Verify that all male attendants have been measured for their formalwear.

It's two months until the wedding.

- 🍂 Choose your wedding rings.
- 🍂 Conclude all honeymoon plans.
- 🍂 Finalize and verify details with all service providers.
- 🍂 Mail the invitations.
- 🍂 Obtain accessory items such as a purse, shoes, the ring bearer's pillow, goblets, candles, a guest book, a cake knife, and a garter.
- 🍂 Order the wedding cake.
- 🍂 Plan the bridesmaids' luncheon.

It's six weeks before the big day.

- ❦ Confirm that transportation arrangements have been made for all attendants and out-of-town guests on the wedding day.
- ❦ Discuss wedding photographs with the photographer.
- ❦ Formulate the final menu decisions.
- ❦ Have your formal bridal portrait done.
- ❦ Make sure all attendants are aware of the time, location, and date of the wedding rehearsal and dinner afterward.
- ❦ Pick up your gown.
- ❦ Verify that all male and female attendants have been fitted for their formalwear.

There are two weeks left to go.

- ❦ Address formal announcements.
- ❦ Arrange for someone to say grace before dinner.
- ❦ Complete blood and medical tests.
- ❦ Confirm accommodations for out-of-town guests.
- ❦ Have your bridesmaids' luncheon.
- ❦ Keep records of gifts as they arrive.
- ❦ Make a seating chart for the reception.
- ❦ Obtain the marriage license (or refer to local regulations).
- ❦ Preaddress envelopes for thank-you notes to guests.
- ❦ Prepare a wedding announcement for the newspaper.
- ❦ Provide the musicians with a list of your musical selections.
- ❦ Write thank-you notes immediately upon receiving gifts.

The wedding is in one week!

- ❦ Confirm details with all professional services.
- ❦ Give the final guest count for the reception meal to your caterer.
- ❦ Make a list of names and their pronunciation for the best man to mention in his introduction.
- ❦ Make sure that the marriage license has been picked up.

- Pick up your wedding rings.
- Prepare a ceremony seating list for ushers (if necessary).
- Present the attendants with their gifts.
- Verify that all of your attendants have picked up and tried on their dresses.

Tomorrow is your wedding day!

- Attend the wedding rehearsal and the rehearsal dinner.
- Inventory everything you will need for tomorrow and make sure you have it handy.
- Distribute the attendants' gifts if you haven't already done so.
- Review any special ceremony seating arrangements with ushers.
- Tell attendants to arrive at your home about one hour before you'll leave for the ceremony site if you'll be having pictures taken there.

It's your wedding day!

- Allow yourself plenty of time to get ready.
- Leave early for the ceremony site.
- Try to stay calm.

You're married!

- Leave for your honeymoon.
- Mail announcements.

It's one month after the wedding.

- By now you should have all of your thank-you notes written and mailed.

3

SOME ASSEMBLY REQUIRED:

THE WEDDING PARTY

What is the minimum number of attendants I should have?

Two witnesses to the ceremony to sign the marriage license.

How do I know how many attendants to have?

Your personal preference and the size and style of wedding are the foundations for the decision. Traditionally, very formal weddings have up to twelve female attendants. Less formal ceremonies average about six; smaller, semiformal or informal weddings, from two to four; and very small informal celebrations, one attendant each.

Whom do I ask?

Close family members and closest friends are usually those asked to participate. Often if the groom has a sister, the bride includes her in her party of attendants. The groom does the same if the bride has a brother.

If I was in their wedding, must I ask them to be in mine?

No. They might have a small family, where you have a large one. In any case, you are not obligated to reciprocate.

What if people I asked keep complaining about the costs? I've asked a few people to be in my wedding party, and they keep mentioning how expensive it all is. Should I offer them the option of bowing out?

Have the dresses been selected and ordered? Will it upset a particular balance in the party? If it will mean true financial hardship, yes. However, since most people know that joining a wedding party incurs financial obligations, they might just be blowing off steam.

Must the number of bridesmaids and groomsmen be equal?

No. But it shouldn't be severely unbalanced. A wedding party with eight bridesmaids and two groomsmen would look unusual.

What is the difference between the *maid* and *matron of honor*?

A *maid* is not married and a *matron* is or has been married.

What is an *honor attendant*?

A newer, more politically correct way of saying *maid* or *matron of honor* or *best man*. Some brides choose a male friend as their honor attendant; some grooms choose a female friend as their honor attendant.

May I have two honor attendants? I can't choose between my sisters.

Some brides have two and divide the duties among them. More

than two might result in confusion because the honor attendant has a lot of responsibilities. It would take major coordination to make sure they weren't relying on the other to do the tasks. In addition, you can choose only one to sign the registry certificate as official witness to the ceremony.

I set my wedding date a year ahead of time. Now my matron of honor has announced that she will be about eight months pregnant at the wedding. She has offered me the option of her bowing out, but I know she was looking forward to being my honor attendant. Any suggestions?

The same thing happened to me, and she had the baby two weeks before the wedding! If you like, you might choose to have two honor attendants. That will take some of the load off your current matron of honor. The second attendant can also serve as a backup if your friend has her baby early!

May I ask my mother to be my honor attendant?

It's a nice idea, but, as the official hostess of the wedding, she'll have too many other responsibilities.

Should all the female attendants be the same general age? I'm thirty-two. My matron of honor is near my age, as are two of the bridesmaids. The other bridesmaids are all much younger cousins, in their teens. Several people have told me everyone in the wedding party should be close to my age. Is that true?

The custom of the wedding attendants being near the age of the bride evolved for practical reasons. They are her support system, and it is logical that attendants much older or much younger may not provide the support the bride needs. In your case, you have several people to assist you as needed. There doesn't seem to be any perceptible reason why your teenage cousins shouldn't participate, too.

Why aren't married bridesmaids called *bridesmatrons*?

Although the distinction is made for the honor attendant (maid of honor, matron of honor), it is not made for the other attendants. No matter what their marital status, they are bridesmaids.

Do I have to include a bridesmaid's spouse in the wedding party?

No. If you are also close friends with her husband it is definitely a nice gesture but not necessary. However, the spouse of all your attendants would be invited to the wedding, rehearsal dinner, and reception.

What is a *junior bridesmaid?*

A young girl from ten to fourteen years of age. She can dress the same as the other bridesmaids or slightly different. It's entirely optional whether you would assign a groomsman to escort her.

What is the maximum age for a ring bearer or flower girl?

After the age of ten, the child would be an usher or junior bridesmaid. Also, children participating in the wedding shouldn't be younger than four. Younger children tend to become confused and frightened by all the excitement and attention.

Must I have a ring bearer and a flower girl?

No. They are traditional but not necessary. They add a cute touch to the day, but both roles are entirely ceremonial.

What is a *page?*

When the bride's gown has an extremely long train, young boys between the ages of four and ten help to carry it in the processional.

What is the difference between an *usher* and a *groomsman?*

This role is often combined. By definition, an usher seats the guests at the wedding ceremony while a groomsman escorts a bridesmaid in the processional and recessional. You need one usher to seat every fifty guests. You can assume one-half to three-fourths of your invited guests will attend the ceremony.

Can my fiancé's father be his best man?

Yes. He'll probably be very honored, and he should be very reliable in that role.

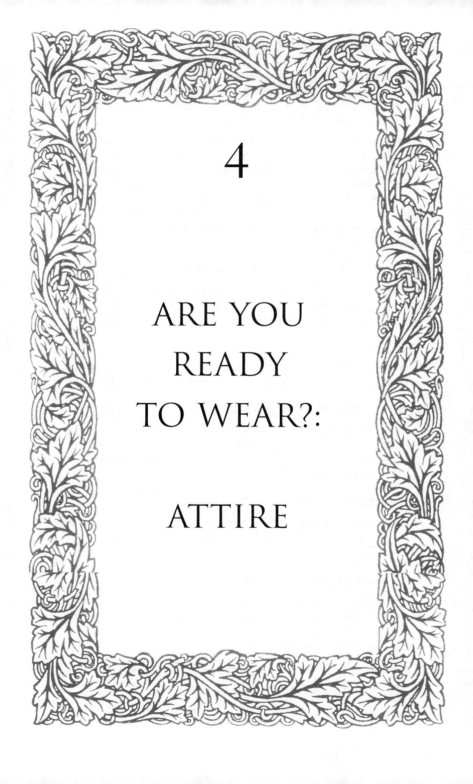

4

ARE YOU
READY
TO WEAR?:

ATTIRE

Can I Wear Velvet in July?: Bride Attire

Who must I take with me to select my gown and headpiece? I would like to go shopping for my gown alone. However, my mother, sister, maid of honor, and future mother-in-law all seem to think they should join me. Whom am I required to take? I don't want a circus!

You aren't required to bring anyone along. And you're right: Too many people accompanying you could result in mass confusion, conflicting opinions, and disagreements. However, selecting your gown will be difficult, and you may be surprised at the emotions it evokes. I would suggest bringing at least one person along. Your mother is the obvious choice. If she is unable or if you just don't get along, your maid of honor is the traditional second choice. Many brides bring both to help with the selection.

What should I wear to a formal daytime wedding?

A white or ivory floor-length gown with a train and formal matching headwear with a long veil would be appropriate. If the gown is sleeveless or short-sleeved, you would wear long gloves.

A formal evening wedding?

If your wedding takes place after 6 P.M., you and your attendants would generally have more elaborate fabrics and ornamentation.

Somewhere between formal and informal?

The term for this is *semiformal*. Your gown can still be ankle or floor length. Fabrics and ornamentation are less sophisticated and ornate. The train (if any) is quite short, and the veil is seldom longer than the elbow.

Must I wear a veil if I have a church wedding?

No, unless it is a requirement of your particular church. Your veil depends on the style of headpiece you have chosen and your own wishes in the matter.

What is the longest veil I may wear?

It's a matter of personal preference. If you are wearing a very formal gown, your veil is usually fairly long. If you are wearing a

large cap or hat, the veil is usually shorter.

What length of veil would I wear with a knee-length dress?

It shouldn't be any longer than your chin.

Why do women wear face (blusher) veils?

You don't, unless it's required by the religious denomination you are marrying through. Historically, a face veil was used for arranged marriages. The groom didn't know what the bride looked like until he married her and lifted the veil. Most brides who use blusher veils today just like the custom and choose to follow it.

Am I too old to wear a veil?

An older bride does not customarily wear a veil. However, if it means that much to you, go ahead and wear one.

Would a widow or divorcée wear a veil?

Divorcées and widows do not wear veil headpieces unless they are required by their religious traditions.

When should I wear gloves?

The only time they must be worn is if your wedding style is very formal.

How do I know what kind of gloves to wear?

They should enhance your overall look by blending with the style, fabric, and ornamentation of your gown. If you are wearing a long-sleeved dress, your gloves should end at the wrist. Gloves covering the entire arm look best with a sleeveless gown.

How do I take gloves off smoothly during the exchange of rings?

You can have just the ring finger slit or wear fingerless gloves.

What shoe style should I wear?

If you have a long, sweeping train, wear pumps. With a knee-length gown, wear heels.

What material should the shoes be made of? Do my wedding shoes have to be covered with fabric?

Shoes should match the style and color of your dress. They may be covered with richly ornamented fabrics or topped with satin rosettes, jewels, lace, bows, sequins, or rhinestones. Leather shoes are considered street shoes and only appropriate for the most casual weddings.

What jewelry should I wear?

It depends on the style of your dress and the formality of your wedding. Pearls are a very traditional choice, as is a simple gold locket. Some brides like to combine elements of the gown's ornamentation—such as beads, crystals, seed pearls—into their jewelry. Most important, keep it simple.

Can I wear white if I've been married before?

Yes. White was once supposed to be indicative of a bride's virginity. Now, it is just the traditional color for the bride's garments.

What is the most traditional and formal fabric for wedding gowns?

Satin in the winter, taffeta or lace in the spring, chiffon or organdy in the summer, and brocade or velvet in the fall.

My best friend is lending me her gown but refuses to take money for it. What should I do?

You are very fortunate to have such a trusting friend. Take good care of the gown. Have it cleaned and packaged before returning it to her. Send her a thank-you letter and some sort of gift. A small, personal item will be ideal.

Why Do I Have to Wear a Penguin Suit?: Groom Attire

What would a groom wear to a formal daytime wedding?

His jacket style might be tailcoat cutaway, stroller, or tuxedo. Trousers would match or contrast the jacket. He'd wear a white shirt with a wing collar and French cuffs. Traditionally, the cummerbund and vest match. Ascot or striped ties. Accessories such as top hats and gloves are optional.

A formal evening wedding?

A formal wedding after 6 P.M. is the most elaborate wedding style. A wing-collared shirt, bow tie, and a full-dress tailcoat with matching trousers and waistcoat is the traditional male attire.

A semiformal daytime wedding?

The groom would wear a white shirt, four-in-hand tie or ascot, and a gray cutaway coat with matching striped trousers and matching waistcoat or a tuxedo jacket with matching trousers, a cummerbund or waistcoat, and a plain or pleated front shirt and bow tie.

A semiformal evening wedding?

Black or midnight blue tuxedo jacket with matching trousers, a waistcoat or cummerbund, a bow tie, and a plain or pleated front shirt.

What sort of flowers belong in the groom's boutonniere?

They should be one or two that are part of your bouquet.

Cultivating Affordable and Wearable Formalwear: Attendant Attire

Who selects the bridesmaids' dresses?

Because bridesmaids pay for their own apparel, most brides feel it is fair to give them a voice in the selection. But to avoid too much confusion, visit the shop ahead of time and select three or four dresses that you like. Then allow them to choose among those selections.

How do I choose something attractive?

The gowns should be a fabric and style appropriate for the season and occasion. In other words, you wouldn't want cotton gowns in December or heavy taffeta gowns at a summer seaside wedding. Select something that will look most attractive on the body types of your attendants. If they are primarily short and tiny, don't select huge, overwhelming southern-belle gowns. If they are primarily tall and heavy, don't select skintight slinky knits.

What if my attendants do not like the gowns?

The larger the wedding party, the harder it will be to make everyone happy. If you have done your best to select an attractive gown and keep costs down, that's about all you can do. In reality, few bridesmaids like their gowns. If a person strenuously objects, you can offer the option of leaving the wedding party. It is your day, and your choices should prevail. Most friends understand that.

What would my attendants wear to a formal daytime wedding?

Gowns would be floor- or ankle-length and complementary in style, color, and length. Shoes and other accessories would match or blend with the gown.

What would my attendants wear to a formal evening wedding?

They'd wear formal floor-length gowns with matching shoes and they'd wear gloves if the gowns are sleeveless or if you wish them to accessorize with gloves.

Must the bridesmaids' dresses be identical in color?

No; they can be in various hues of the same color (such as light blue to dark blue) or complementary colors such as pale peach, pale yellow, and cream. On occasion, a bride will have each bridesmaid wear a completely different color. Such a wedding is called a rainbow wedding.

How do I match the style of the bridesmaids' dresses to my gown? I keep hearing that the bridesmaids' dresses should match my gown. None of the ones I have seen look anything like my dress.

The advice is referring to choosing gowns that are a similar degree of style and formality and in a fabric that complements yours. In other words, if your gown is a formal, elaborate satin with a two-foot train, you would not select casual knee-length cotton lace dresses for your attendants.

Does the maid of honor wear the same style of dress as the bridesmaids?

Usually her dress is the same or a very similar style. What might differ is the color or her flowers. Some honor attendants wear a different hue than the other bridesmaids. Others might wear a reverse complementary color, such as a deep gold when the others are wearing forest green. Her bouquet might be a reverse of the other attendants' flowers or have ribbons and accents different from the others'.

Should my maid of honor carry flowers different from the bridesmaids'?

She usually carries the same bouquet of flowers. However, sometimes the accent flowers or ribbon decorating the bouquet are in a different color.

May I tell my attendants how to wear their hair?

You may suggest that they wear it a certain way, but you can't order them to do so.

What should the junior bridesmaids wear? The style I like for my attendants' gowns is fairly sophisticated. I have a fourteen-year-old sister who will be a junior bridesmaid. May she wear a different style of gown?

Yes, a complementary or similar style—whether it's the fabric, color, or pattern that's similar—that matches the rest is perfectly appropriate for a junior bridesmaid.

Do I purchase the attendants' jewelry?

No, but you may suggest the type of jewelry you would like to see them wear.

Does the flower girl wear the same headpiece as the bridesmaids?

No. The flower girl's headpiece very rarely is the same as the rest of the female attendants. Many young girls wear ribbons of the wedding colors trailing from a pretty barrette or a wreath of silk flowers. Some wear nothing on their heads at all.

How can an out-of-town groomsman be measured for his tuxedo?

Have the groomsman visit a formalwear shop in his area and ask to be measured. Then, instruct him to send those measurements to your local formalwear shop, and they will reserve the appropriate size clothing.

Must all the men's attire be matching?

Traditionally, all the men in the wedding party wear the same style of clothing, even the groom, except he wears a different boutonniere. Many grooms also select a different color tie and cummerbund to distinguish themselves from the rest.

What should the ring bearer wear?

His clothes should match the clothes of the rest of the men, although he can wear dress shorts or knickers instead of long pants. Or, depending on age and personality, a child under five can dress in matching colors in dressy children's clothing. For example, in a winter wedding velvet shorts and vest with a nice shirt would work very well.

Presentable Clothing: Parent Attire

What should our fathers wear?

The fathers tend to wear black ties and cummerbunds, no matter what the rest of the wedding party is wearing.

Are the dresses for the mother of the bride and the mother of the groom supposed to match?

No. They should, however, be complementary in style and color. For example, his mother in a purple flowing gown and your mother in a sleek orange ensemble would not be complementary.

Should our mothers choose gowns in the same color as the bridesmaids' gowns?

No, they should both choose shades that will match or blend with the colors chosen. The mothers should not wear the same colors, either.

Must the mothers of the bride and groom wear hats?

Only in very formal weddings. On those occasions they might choose a hat with a short veil or decorative flowers.

Should our mothers wear gloves as part of their ensemble?

If it is a very formal wedding, or if everyone else will be wearing gloves, they should also wear gloves.

How do we decide what style of clothing to wear?

The size of the wedding, time of day, location, and formality of your gown determine what everyone else will wear.

5

YOU
ARE
INVITED

Gather Ye Names While Ye May: The Guest List

How do we decide how many people to invite?

That decision will depend on your budget and the style of your wedding.

Is there a formula to determine whom to invite, such as only first cousins or friends you have known for at least a year?

If you can, you should include all the people you would truly miss if they weren't there.

I'm having a large wedding. Several acquaintances of mine seem to assume they'll be invited. There really isn't room. Should I explain or just invite them anyway?

Because weddings are joyful, celebratory events, many people like to attend, but you should not let such assumptions affect your plans. Some people might assume they'll be invited, but no one has a right to an invitation.

If I've been married before may I invite the same guests?

Invite them! If you are still close to them, they will surely rejoice in your second chance at happiness.

What if I receive a gift from someone I am not planning to invite? My aunt's neighbor gave us a beautiful gift. I wasn't planning to invite her, but now my aunt says I must. This will only offend other people I'm not able to invite. Should I return the gift?

No, that would be offensive. Send her a thank-you note for the gift. Add an explanation that you are sorry you cannot extend an invitation to the wedding because the guest list is limited. Suggest having a get-together for lunch or dinner after the wedding.

Should I invite two aunts who don't speak? If I don't invite them both to the shower and to the wedding, it will cause further hurt feelings among the family. But I don't want their anger ruining my celebrations. I've talked to them, and they both said they would just ignore the other. My grandmother doesn't think that is possible. What should I do?

Invite them both to the shower. If they can't control themselves, wouldn't you prefer to find out then rather than on your wedding day?

Do I send invitations to the people in the wedding party? What about the clergyperson?

Yes, send invitations to all. Invitations are also keepsakes of the occasion. Your clergyperson should also receive an invitation if you wish for him or her to join the reception celebration.

Do we have to allow each single friend to bring a guest? If we have to, it will destroy our budget. Is that required?

No. If someone is engaged or part of a well-established couple, that person's partner should be included if possible. In that case, his or her partner's name would be written out on the envelope as well.

Is there anything wrong with bulletin board invitations? I work in a small company of twenty-eight people. Rather than mail all those invitations, I put one up on the bulletin board inviting everyone to come and celebrate. A coworker has informed me that several are not attending because they feel that such an invitation is just a token way of inviting people and that they aren't really welcome. How can I prove her wrong?

Every invited guest should receive an invitation. If you can't afford to send one to each, then you should cut back on your wedding. Bulletin board invitations are generally considered an invitation to the ceremony only. No gift is expected of someone who attends from such an invitation. At this point, you can explain the misunderstanding to your coworkers. But you can't prove them wrong, because they are not.

What percentage of those invited will probably attend?

Generally, 75 percent will attend. But the number can be affected by adverse weather, summer vacations, and other activities that may conflict with your wedding date.

Does the bride's family get to invite more guests?

No. Although the bride's family traditionally sets the size of the guest list, the groom's family may use half the allotted slots.

What if the groom's family is bigger than the bride's?

Traditionally, it doesn't matter whose family is larger. If two hundred guests will be invited, his family has the option of inviting one hundred. But if your family genuinely doesn't need to invite half of the guests, it would be nice if you let the groom's family invite more than half of the guests.

We're inviting 250 guests. My guest list keeps growing and growing. How do I stop this?

This is a common problem with large weddings. Everyone understands the limits to a small gathering. But a big wedding is a big occasion. Your mother has probably talked about the wedding with the members of her bridge club for the past six months. They feel so much like part of the planning to her, she now wants them to be part of the celebration. Your fiancé's mother may have done the same with her friends at work. How do you stop these friends from being added to the guest list? Have a talk with your mom. Remind her that this is your big day, and although you appreciate her enthusiasm and desire to share it with people she cares about, you want to stop any further additions to the guest list. Suggest that she invite these friends to a small gathering a few weeks after the wedding where they can express their happiness to you and your new spouse.

I have fifteen cousins, but I'm close to only three of them. My mother says if I want to invite those three, I must invite all fifteen. Must I invite all relatives of equal rank if I invite one of them?

It depends on your family. In some families, if you don't invite them all, it will start a family feud. Even if the cousins themselves don't care, their parents might be offended.

I haven't spoken to my cousin in eight years. Must I invite a close relative if I'm not speaking to her?

A wedding is a family celebration. Deliberately leaving one person out of the picture has potential for creating hurt feelings. Talk to her mother. If her mother understands your feelings, then it's up to you. If she prefers that you invite her, offer the invitation as an olive branch. And if your cousin refuses to come, well, you tried, didn't you?

I'm very close to my ten-year-old niece; I want to invite her to the wedding but not any other children—especially my other sister's wild children. Since I'm not close to the other children, may I just invite the children I like?

No, unless your ten-year-old niece is in the wedding party. Traditionally, children in the wedding party and brothers and sisters of the bride and groom are always invited. After that, if you invite one child, you must invite all children of guests.

I have quite a few relatives that live on the other side of the country. I know they won't be able to attend the wedding. It seems wrong to send them an invitation; they might think I just want them to send a gift. Should I send invitations to people when I know they cannot come?

Yes. If you don't, they will feel left out, which is clearly not your intention. Let them decide if they want to send you a gift. And you never know; they just may be able to attend.

My maid of honor asked me for a guest list for the shower. Is every woman who is invited to the wedding also invited to the shower?

You do not need to invite every woman on the wedding guest list to your shower. Generally, you invite those you are closest to: your grandmothers' sisters and their daughters, your parents' sisters (or sisters-in-law) and their daughters, friends, neighbors, coworkers, and cousins with whom you are close.

How can I trim the guest list?

It's easiest to make a rule—for example, no neighbors, third cousins, or coworkers—that applies to both families.

I have several distant cousins who had very large weddings. I am having a much smaller gathering, but my mother insists that I must invite them, because they invited me to theirs. Must I invite all relatives who invited me to their weddings?

No, but you might want to drop them a note explaining that you are having a smaller affair.

My mother says that if my father comes, she is staying home. What should I do?

It's frustrating when adults act like children, and weddings often bring out emotions and childishness that are otherwise kept hidden. It is your wedding and you should not give in to such emotional blackmail. If your mother would truly stay away from your wedding over such an issue, she doesn't deserve to be there. However, in most cases like this, once people realize that emotional blackmail will not work, they abandon their misguided attitudes.

My fiancé's mother has decided to wear black because she doesn't approve of me. Should we tell her to stay home?

Too often, what should be a day of celebration turns into a day of emotional banner waving. Let her come. Think how ridiculous she will look in the wedding pictures when you display them at your twenty-fifth anniversary party.

Although my husband died several years ago, our children and I have remained very close to his family. My fiancé gets along very well with them, too. My mother says that it is insulting to my fiancé's family to invite my first husband's parents and siblings to our wedding. I would like very much to invite them, and I know it would mean a lot to my children to have them there. My fiancé says that he doesn't mind. Is my mother right?

It is wonderful that you have stayed close to his family. Having them join the celebration would definitely help your children understand that they are not losing one family, but gaining another. Ask your fiancé to talk with his parents to ensure there is no misunderstanding and hard feelings. You should also discuss the idea with your first husband's parents. As much as they may wish you joy, it might also be extremely painful for them to watch you marry and recall a previous wedding day.

The Honor of Their Presence: Invitations

How do I decide what style of invitations to use?

It's based on a combination of personal preference and the style of wedding you'll be having. A thick, white, richly engraved invitation announces a very formal wedding. A handwritten note or computer-generated card implies a small, informal gathering.

Where do I find wedding invitations?

There are large sample catalogs available in bridal shops, some department stores, florists, photographers, print shops, and any other location involved in the wedding trade. Invitations are also available through mail-order catalogs. You can find the names and addresses of these companies in any bridal magazine.

What does a traditional, formal invitation look like?

It's on thick, quality paper in cream or ivory and has a plain design, with, at most, a simple border. Text appears on the front, engraved in thick, black ink.

Are the invitations always issued by the bride's parents?

Traditionally, yes, even if they aren't contributing to the expenses. An older bride (especially one who has been married before) might wish to issue the invitation in her and her fiancé's name, but it's not necessary. If circumstances won't allow the bride's parents to be the hosts, the invitations may be issued by a guardian, a friend, or the bride and groom. Sometimes the groom's parents are included on the invitation, but that's entirely optional.

What if I'm an older bride and this is my second wedding?

An older bride and her fiancé have the option of issuing the invitation in their names. Or, the bride's parents are always able to issue the invitation in their names.

Why do invitations always say "the honor of your presence"?

Invitations don't always say it; nevertheless, that is the traditional wording for invitations to the church ceremony.

What is the traditional way of wording an invitation to the wedding reception?

The invitation says "*request the pleasure of your company.*"

If it is a double wedding, which bride's name is first on the invitation?

The elder bride's name would be first.

If I'm a doctor, does that designation belong on the invitation?

Traditionally, it appears only if you and your groom are issuing the invitation.

What kind of doctor must I be to include the doctor designation on the invitation?

A doctor of medicine or doctor of theology would be designated as *doctor*. A person with an academic doctorate would not use the title of *doctor*.

What is the traditional invitation wording?

> *Mr. and Mrs. David Carter Francis*
> *request the honor of your presence*
> *at the marriage of their daughter*
> *Elizabeth Ann*
> *to*
> *Daniel George Bailey*
> *on*
> *Saturday, the ninth of August*
> *Two thousand and three*
> *at four o'clock*
> *Congregational Reformed Church*
> *12 East State Street*
> *Providence, Rhode Island*

What is the correct wording for an invitation issued in special situations?

Bride's mother is widowed:

> *Mrs. Wade Kendall*
> *requests the honor of your presence*
> *at the marriage of her daughter*
> *Marilyn Kay Kendall*
> *to*
> *Edwin Paul Cusick*
> *on*
> *Saturday, the third of November*
> *Two thousand and five*
> *at one o'clock*
> *Holy Family Catholic Church*
> *841 New Mountain Highway*
> *Palos Heights, Wyoming*

Bride's parents are both divorced and remarried; invitation is issued by her parents alone:

> *Mrs. David Sheppard*
> *and*
> *Mr. Tyler P. Fahrezee*
> *request the pleasure of your company*
> *at the marriage of their daughter*
> *Sharon Grace Fahrezee*
> *to*
> *Joseph Michael Peitrellio*
> *on*
> *Friday, the first of February*
> *Two thousand and eight*
> *at four o'clock*
> *Farmington Hills Opera House*
> *923 Pavilion Road*
> *Rivertown, Ohio*

Bride's parents are both divorced and remarried; invitation is issued to include stepparents:

> *Mr. and Mrs. Francis Larierre*
> *and*
> *Mr. and Mrs. Michael P. McNair*
> *request the pleasure of your company*
> *at the marriage of their daughter*
> *Jennifer Lynn McNair*
> *to*
> *David Francis Linn*
> *on*
> *Saturday, the eighth of May*
> *Two thousand and eight*
> *at eleven o'clock*
> *First Congregational Church*
> *1001 Moran Street*
> *Bridgeman, Connecticut*

Bride's stepmother and father issue the invitation:

Mr. and Mrs. Chan Wong
request the honor of your presence
at the marriage of Mrs.
Wong's stepdaughter
Catherine Pearl
to
Kao Nayimoto
on
Sunday, the seventh of June
Nineteen and ninety-eight
at two-thirty in the afternoon
Wildwood Lake Park
Rogers Road
Sausalito, California

Both the bride's parents and
the groom's parents issue the invitation:

Mr. and Mrs. Richard H. Bowers
request the honor of your presence
at the marriage of their daughter
Kara Lee
to
Mr. Jason Wright Hartman
son of Mr. and Mrs. Cyrus T. Hartman
on
Monday, the fourth of July
Two thousand and ten
at four o'clock
Crooked Tree Country Club
1189 Bluehill Drive
Bennington, Kentucky

The groom's parents issue the invitation:

Mr. and Mrs. Roberto J. Hernandez
request the honor of your presence
at the marriage of
Victoria Sophia Vasquez
to their son
Mr. Jose Juan Hernandez
on
Saturday, the twelfth of August
Two thousand and six
at five-thirty in the afternoon
St. James Episcopal Church
9547 Cecily Road
Houston, Texas

The bride and groom issue the invitation:

The honor of your presence
is requested at the marriage of
Miss Bridget Erin Reilly
to
Mr. Walter Paul Kelorchak
on
Saturday, the first of September
Two thousand and five
at four o'clock
Mullet Grace Gardens
821 Lakeshore Drive
Poulsbo, Washington

The bride and groom issue the invitation;
bride is a doctor:

> *The honor of your presence*
> *is requested*
> *at the marriage of*
> *Dr. Valerie Teresa Kwalsi*
> *to*
> *Mr. Richard Dean Demko*
> *Sunday, the eleventh of May*
> *Two thousand and one*
> *at six o'clock in the evening*
> *First Presbyterian Church*
> *53 Chestnut Drive*
> *Baytown, Massachusetts*

The bride's parents issue the invitation; bride's
mother is a doctor:

> *Dr. Susan and Mr. Robert Keelston*
> *request the honor of your presence*
> *at the marriage of their daughter*
> *Samantha Jane Keelston*
> *to*
> *Mr. Zachary T. Nolan*
> *Friday, the twenty-fifth of June*
> *Two thousand and eight*
> *at half past six o'clock*
> *Our Savior Lutheran Church*
> *5224 Magnolia Street*
> *Newport, Rhode Island*

Double wedding invitation where the brides are not sisters:

Mr. and Mrs. Albert K. Fox
and
Mr. and Mrs. John R. Ramsey
request the honor of your presence
at the marriage of their daughters
Felicia Marie Fox
to
Mr. Jeffrey Allan Sims
and
Kelly Ann Ramsey
to
Mr. Robert Stephen Krga
Saturday, the tenth of August
Two thousand and seven
at half past five o'clock
Hyatt Regency Hotel
12422 Highway 11 South
Grand Forks, North Dakota

Double wedding invitation of sisters:

Mr. and Mrs. Jerome William Davis
request the honor of your presence
at the marriage of their daughters
Catherine Joyce
to
Mr. Tyler John Wilson
and
Sharon Grace
to
Mr. Carter David Francis
Saturday, the eleventh of April
Two thousand and seven
at half past four o'clock
United Methodist Church
8214 Old Turtle Creek Boulevard
Sante Fe, New Mexico

Wedding ceremony and reception on one invitation:

> *Mr. and Mrs. Jacob E. Nolan*
> *request the honor of your presence*
> *at the marriage of their daughter*
> *Tabitha Elaine*
> *to*
> *Mr. Paul K. Richards*
> *Saturday, the sixth of July*
> *Two thousand and two*
> *at half after seven o'clock*
> *United Methodist Church*
> *Seventh and Main Streets*
> *and afterward at the reception*
> *Willow Hills Country Club*
> *350 Forest Hill Lane*
> *The favor of a reply is requested*
> *2323 Vine Lane*
> *Pittsburgh, Pennsylvania*

Small, informal wedding:

If there are fewer than fifty guests, a short, handwritten note with the necessary information is all that is needed. Here is an example:

> Dear Travis and Rita,
>
> Rebecca and Kyle will be married at 8 P.M. Friday, April 16th, at Marquette Park. A small reception will follow.
>
> Please join us for this happy occasion.
>
> Love,
>
> Cheryl and Dan

My father died when I was young. My grandmother should be included on the announcement and on the in mean to be flip, but how can a deceased person invite pee wedding? Should his name be on the invitations?

It's understandable that your grandmother wants your father to be a part of your wedding but only the living can announce something or issue an invitation.

Do I need to enclose a reception card with my invitation?

The tradition of inviting some people to the ceremony and others to the reception is not as common today. Most guests are invited to both, and reception information is included on the same invitation as the ceremony. The primary exception would be for very formal weddings, which follow tradition much more closely.

What is the traditional reception card wording?

The card is issued by the same party that issues the wedding invitations. Here is an example:

Mr. and Mrs. Arthur K. Partello
request the pleasure of your company
on Saturday, the third of August
Two thousand and four
at half after six o'clock in the evening
Bay Harbor Yacht Club
11 Lakeshore Road
Portland, Maine

Should I send response cards? I think they make it easy for guests to inform you if they are coming. However, etiquette books say that these should not be included. Why?

In theory, everyone who you invite should know that they are expected to make a written response to your invitation as soon as possible. Most etiquette experts consider it insulting to your guests to do the work for them by including a response card. In reality, these cards have become customary in many regions and guests rely on them to respond.

How would I add reception information to the ceremony invitation?

If you will have the same guests at both, you might add the information to the bottom left-hand corner. If they will take

n, it might read:

ion following the ceremony

e at a different location it might read:

Reception at six o'clock
Lake Timberland Pavilion
19 Kingsridge Drive
Wendalla, Oregon

Why shouldn't I address my invitations through my computer? My mother insists that they be addressed by hand. Why?

Historically, invitations were addressed by hand because there was no other option. The practice has continued because it offers a personal touch. Also, only blue or black ink is used. Preprinted labels are associated with junk mail and are not considered suitable for an occasion as dignified as a wedding.

How should I assemble the envelopes? How do I address the inner and outer envelopes?

The inner envelope lists those actually invited to the wedding. Traditionally, if a person's name is not on it, he or she isn't invited. On both envelopes, all names are completely written out. No abbreviations are used. If children are less than sixteen years of age, they would have their names written on the inner envelope if they are invited. Anyone over sixteen should receive his or her own invitation.

How do I address invitations in special circumstances?

We do not want children to attend:

Do not write their names on the inner envelope.

The pleasure of your company is requested
at a reception for adults
at four-thirty in the evening
Monroe Pavilion
759 Remington Drive
Helena, Montana

To a married couple:

The outer envelope would read their full married names without abbreviation in the names.

Mr. and Mrs. Frederick Paul Rodgers

The inner envelope would read Mr. and Mrs. Rodgers.

A married couple in which the wife has kept her maiden name:

The outer envelope would list both full names, alphabetically.

Ms. Rhonda Joan Kellerman
Mr. Joshua Ashford St. Clair

The inner envelope would read

Ms. Kellerman
Mr. St. Clair

To a single person and his or her guest:

Learn the guest's name and include it on the envelope.

You should not write "*and Guest*" because a wedding isn't the same as a concert ticket. A person participating in your celebration should be someone you know. If a friend is bringing a date, you should at least know the date's name.

To a single person and no guest:

Simply write that person's name on the envelope. Don't add anything else.

Why is there white tissue paper with the invitations?

Historically, it was to keep the ink from the engraving from smearing. Now many follow the custom because they're used to seeing it that way.

What is the traditional way to assemble the invitations?

Place any enclosure cards and maps inside the invitation. Put the invitation in the inner envelope fold-side down. The print side faces the back flap. Do not seal the inner envelope. Place the inner envelope inside the outer envelope. The front side, where the names are written, should face the outer envelope's back flap. Seal the outer envelope.

When should I mail invitations?

Six to eight weeks before your wedding date.

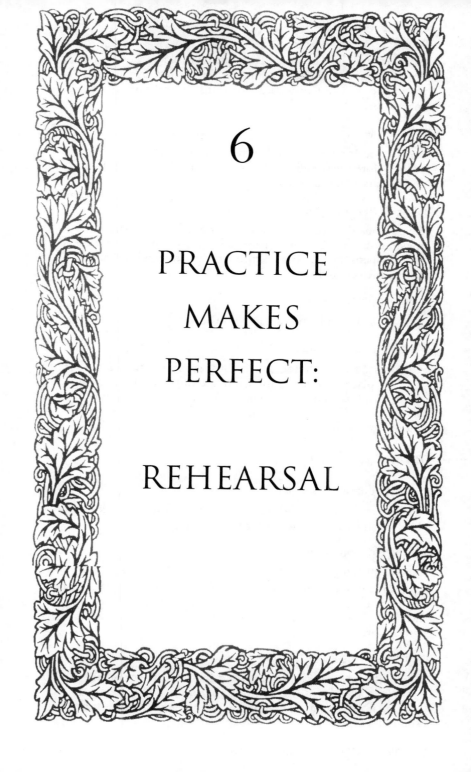

6

PRACTICE
MAKES
PERFECT:

REHEARSAL

Why do we need a rehearsal?

Everyone will be a bit anxious about their role in the ceremony. Your officiant can help ease some of this anxiety by running through duties and answering questions. In addition, practice makes perfect!

Who schedules it?

You or your fiancé should. It is not automatically set for the night before the wedding, just traditionally. Be sure to discuss the rehearsal and date with your officiant.

Must everyone in the wedding party attend?

If at all possible, yes. Sometimes extenuating circumstances make it unavoidable for a bridesmaid or usher not to be there. If that happens, be sure to run through their roles with them before the ceremony.

Should our parents attend?

Yes. They should be there if at all possible.

Our photographer wants to attend. Should we let her?

Chances are your photographer is just scouting the location for the best places to photograph from, looking over the wedding party for ideas, and getting a general feel for the next day's activities. Unless your officiant objects, there is no reason she should not be there.

Rehearsal Dinner

Who hosts the rehearsal dinner?

The groom's family. Traditionally, it is their way of thanking the bride's family for providing for the wedding.

Must the dinner be formal?

Not at all. This is supposed to be a relaxing get-together the night before the more formal affair. Anything from a pizza party to a sit-down four-course meal is acceptable. It is all based on what the groom's parents can provide and what the bride and groom prefer.

Whom should we invite?

Invite the entire wedding party and their significant others, parents and siblings of the bride and groom, child attendants and their parents, and, if you like, the officiant and his or her spouse.

My bridesmaids wish to bring dates to the rehearsal dinner. Would it be wrong to say no?

Members of the wedding party who are married, officially engaged, or who have been in a long live-in relationship should be allowed to bring their significant others. For anyone else, it is the decision of the groom's parents whether they want to incur the additional financial obligation. You, as the bride, can give your opinion one way or another, but they are the official hosts.

Should we invite child attendants? What about their parents?

Yes and yes. In most cases, the parents are already attending because of their close ties to the bride or groom. If it is a long, formal affair they seldom stay for the entire evening.

Should we invite out-of-town guests?

It isn't required. It's a nice gesture if there are just a few people to include. However, if half of your guests are from out of town, the rehearsal dinner could upstage the wedding.

Should we send invitations?

It is not necessary to put anything in writing because this is usually a small, informal affair. However, an informal invitation can be sent if preferred—or if some of your guests are especially forgetful.

Should we predetermine the menu?

The wise host would set the menu to avoid an astronomical bill.

May we ask our guests to pay for their own alcoholic beverages?

Absolutely not. It's not very nice to invite people for dinner and then ask them to pay for their refreshments.

Are there any special traditions to observe during the dinner?

The groom's parents welcome the guests, and then the groom's father makes the first toast. He should express happiness at his son's marriage. The bride's father offers a toast expressing happiness at his daughter's marriage. Usually everyone in the wedding party offers a toast. There are many anecdotes and jokes shared about the happy couple. Sometimes a few creative friends compose a humorous poem or song. Also, the bride and groom often distribute gifts to their attendants on this occasion.

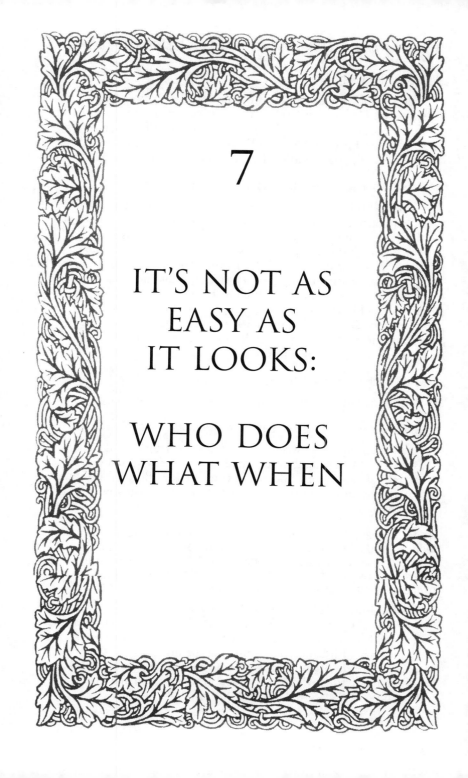

7

IT'S NOT AS EASY AS IT LOOKS:

WHO DOES WHAT WHEN

Paying the Piper: Monetary Responsibilities

Who pays for what?

Traditionally, the bride's parents paid most of the wedding expenses. However, nowadays the financial arrangements are more flexible. Many couples pay for the entire affair themselves. Others fund it through a combination of contributors including both sets of parents and relatives on both sides of the family.

What is a sponsor? How many sponsors should I have?

Customs and traditions have relaxed in the past generation. Where once the wedding bills were entirely the responsibility of the bride's family, it is now acceptable for others to assist in paying for the wedding. A sponsor is somebody who provides financial assistance. Unfortunately, the concept of having sponsors has occasionally been twisted into taking pledges and begging contributions from friends, family, coworkers, and neighbors to help defray the cost of the celebration. Asking for money for any wedding or marriage-related item from anyone except the bride's parents is rude. You may accept money, but you may never ask or hint for it.

How do I ask my rich relative to help pay for the wedding?

You don't. Such contributions must be entirely voluntary.

What if my parents refuse to pay for the wedding I want?

Having an expensive wedding is not an entitlement you were born with. You should never try to have a wedding that costs more than your contributors can comfortably afford. You should pay the remainder of the cost yourself or trim down your expenses.

I'm thirty years old and have never been married before. My fiancé feels we should still expect my parents to pay for the wedding and if they don't that we should issue invitations in our own names. My parents have offered to contribute, but feel I'm old enough to pay my own expenses. I don't want to hurt anyone's feelings. What should I do?

The tradition of placing the bride's parents as hosts of the wedding is not based on financial contributions. The custom evolved from the days when the bride went from her parent's home to her husband's home. Issuing the invitation in their name is an important honor to some parents. If they don't mind whose name the invitation is issued in, then you make that decision. Your age should have nothing to do with it.

A friend at work said that many couples raise money to help pay for their reception by having a benefit dinner and inviting their friends. I've never heard of such a thing. May we hold a benefit dinner to raise money for our wedding?

No, doing so would be ill-mannered. The purpose of a wedding is to invite others to share your happiness on the joyful day of joining your lives together. It's not necessary to shake down your friends to make sure that you have the biggest, most expensive party.

If we are just having a small restaurant dinner after our ceremony, may we ask our guests to pay?

No. Unlike just asking a group of friends out for a meal, a wedding is a special occasion. You pay the bill for anyone you invite to celebrate with you.

What is the bride responsible for financially?

- Groom's wedding ring
- Any physical examination and medical tests required
- A luncheon for the female attendants and gifts for them
- Accommodations for any out-of-town residents

What is the groom responsible for financially?

- Bride's engagement and wedding rings
- The marriage license
- The cost of any examinations and medical tests required
- Bride's bouquet and going-away corsage, as well as flowers for both mothers, himself, male attendants, and honored male guests
- Gifts for the male attendants and their accommodations if they are from out of town
- Wedding officiant's fee

What are the financial responsibilities of the bride's parents?

- Wedding invitations and announcements (including postage and any other related fees)
- Bride's wedding gown, headpiece, and accessories
- Rental fee for the ceremony and reception sites
- Floral arrangements and decorations for the ceremony and reception sites and flowers for female attendants and honored female guests

- Costs for food, beverages, catering, and wedding cake
- Photographer, videographer, musicians, security, and transportation expenses

What are the financial responsibilities of the groom's parents?

- Their own lodging and travel expenses
- The rehearsal dinner
- Any other expenses they would like to assume

What if my fiancé's parents offer to contribute and my parents are insulted?

Many families are now joining together to pay the wedding expenses. Although the bride's family should never ask for assistance, if the groom's family offers, there is no reason to refuse. It is not necessarily a reflection on their economic status. It is more an outlook of "We're all in this together, so let's pay for it together." But if your parents continue to feel uncomfortable, there is no point in forcing the issue.

If my fiancé's parents contribute financially, should their names appear on the invitations as cohosts?

In many cases they are included, whether or not they contribute financially. Their financial contributions do not obligate the bride's family to list them as cohosts, but it would certainly be a nice gesture.

What should the bride's parents know about their responsibilities?

No matter who pays for various items, the bride's mother and father are traditionally the official host and hostess of the celebration. Before the wedding, they are involved in the planning, hopefully to a degree acceptable to everyone involved. It is customary for the bride's mother to choose her gown first and then inform the groom's mother of the style and color. The groom's mother then chooses hers—ideally in a different color. On the wedding day, the bride's mother is the last person seated before the ceremony begins, if she is not part of the processional. She stands at the head of the receiving line at the reception to greet and introduce the guests.

The bride's father will generally escort the bride to the ceremony site and in the processional. He isn't required to stand in the receiving line. Some dads do; others prefer to circulate. Any other customs vary among cultures. In some ethnic groups it is traditional for him to provide shots of whiskey at the reception.

What should the groom's parents know about their responsibilities?

Once the engagement is announced, they should contact the bride's family to welcome their daughter to their family. When the bride's mother informs her of her attire, the groom's mother should choose something in similar style, length, and complementary color. The night before the ceremony, they host a rehearsal dinner for the wedding party and out-of-town guests. At the reception, the groom's mother stands next to the bride's mother in the receiving line. His father may stand in the line or circulate, whichever he prefers.

My parents are paying for most of the wedding costs, so I feel we should honor their wishes. My fiancé says the final decisions should be ours. Who has the final say in a decision if my parents are paying the bill?

This is your special day, and you should both feel comfortable at your own ceremony and reception. Control over the wedding plans is generally based on tradition, not on who contributes the most money. Thus the bride and groom and then the bride's parents have the greatest say in the decisions.

Birds of a Feather Attend Together: Attendant Responsibilities

What must the attendants pay for?

Their travel expenses, wedding attire, and gifts to the happy couple.

What are the duties of the bride's honor attendant?

She is your assistant and helper through all the preparations. This might include accompanying you on shopping expeditions, helping you to make telephone calls, running errands, assisting you in addressing invitations and announcements, and similar duties. In addition, she usually hosts your personal shower and attends all others if possible.

She also watches over you throughout the wedding day to ensure your clothes, hair, and makeup are picture-perfect. During the ceremony she will hold your bouquet, and if it is a double-ring ceremony, she holds the groom's ring until you need it. She signs the register as one of the two official witnesses of the ceremony. In the receiving line and at the head table, she is on the groom's left. Throughout the reception she stays available to assist as needed. If you change into going-away clothes, she will assist you. She is often dressed a bit differently than the other female attendants.

What if my honor attendant lives far away?

Someone has to step into her shoes. You can cover some of the tasks, and perhaps your mother, an aunt, or other close friends can cover the rest. But it could be very awkward to ask someone else to fulfill your absentee honor attendant's duties without giving her the honor of the title.

May I fire my maid of honor? She has been a big disappointment; she doesn't seem to know what she is supposed to do. How do I politely tell her?

Copy the list of duties in this section and pass it along without comment. She should get the picture. If she doesn't, you might ask a mutual friend to talk to her about some of the tasks she needs to accomplish. It's very difficult to fire any wedding attendant, especially an honor attendant, without permanently damaging your relationship.

How may I include my sons in the wedding? Have you any suggestions for what they might do?

It's nice to want to include your children in the wedding. However, their role should be minimal, especially if their other birth parent is still alive. Children tend to have mixed emotions at such occasions. Although two families are joining, this would not be a good time to make a big production out of it. Merely have them walk with you up to the altar and then sit down with the other close family members.

What are the bridesmaids' duties?

They assist you in the preparations, such as addressing envelopes for the invitations and announcements. They may host a few showers and are expected to attend as many wedding-related activities as possible. They provide backup support at the reception for the bride or hostess as needed.

What should I do if a bridesmaid drops out? One of my bridesmaids has decided to elope, and my wedding is in two weeks. She informed me she won't be back from her honeymoon in time for my wedding. Now, everything is out of balance. May I make her pay for the deposit on the groomsman's tuxedo that she was supposed to stand with?

No, you shouldn't make her pay for the deposit. It wasn't nice of her to abandon her commitment to you. However, agreeing to be a bridesmaid doesn't incur any financial obligations toward anyone else in the wedding party. If she left her dress behind and you have a friend who can wear it, that person may step into her role. If not, there is no rule that there has to be an equal number of bridesmaids and groomsmen. Let him keep his tuxedo and enjoy being part of the wedding party.

My two twelve-year-old nieces will be junior bridesmaids. They are very excited about their role. I do not feel they should be invited to every activity—such as my personal shower. My aunt says I must invite them because they are part of the wedding party. It certainly won't be the party I was hoping to have with them in attendance. Must I invite the junior bridesmaids to everything?

No, that is why they are called *junior bridesmaids*. They would attend a mainstream shower, the rehearsal and dinner, and, of course, wedding day festivities. The decision to invite them to anything else is yours.

What does the flower girl do?

Traditionally, she precedes the bride up the aisle, scattering rose petals. Most ceremony sites forbid this practice, but the flower girl still adds a lovely balance to the wedding. Most girls carry a basket of flowers.

We asked my fiancé's five-year-old niece to be our flower girl. Her mother is insisting that we must pay for her dress. Why should we pay for her dress and for no one else's in the wedding party? My fiancé wants to do it to avoid a family squabble, but it just doesn't seem fair to me. We are on a limited budget and paying most of the wedding expenses ourselves. Who pays for the flower girl's dress?

Being right or wrong doesn't always matter when it comes to weddings. Based on custom and tradition, the parents of the flower girl pay for her attire. When they are not financially able to do so, sometimes the grandparents—or the bride and groom—volunteer to pay. However, your fiancé may be right. It may not be worth a family squabble. It is impossible to win in this sort of situation.

What are the responsibilities of the groom's best man?

As primary male attendant he assists in handling arrangements and details for the groom. He attends prewedding festivities and usually hosts the bachelor party. He reminds the groom to attend to details such as picking up his tuxedo and bringing the ring. He is responsible for getting the groom to the ceremony site on time. He holds the ring during the ceremony and passes it to the groom. He is the other official witness to the marriage certificate. At the reception dinner he serves as master of ceremonies, making introductions and offering the first toast. Also, he often takes care of financial details on the wedding day, such as tipping and paying fees.

8

WHAT IT'S ALL ABOUT:

THE WEDDING CEREMONY

It's Beginning to Look A Lot Like Marriage

How do we choose the officiant? We don't have a particular religious affiliation.

You might choose a minister or judge who is a family friend. Or, attend church services at a few denominations; perhaps you will find a place you both feel comfortable with.

Is it rude to ask the officiant how much he or she charges?

No. It will probably be a relief to the officiant, because he or she will expect to be paid but it is often an awkward subject to introduce. However, many like to refer to the charge as a donation rather than a fee.

My uncle is a clergyman, and our local minister has agreed to let him hold the marriage ceremony at our church. Whom do we pay? It seems like we should give my uncle a fee as officiant—but he might be insulted. However, we are using our minister's church, and we should give him something, too. I can't bring myself to ask either one of them about this.

You would give the same donation to your local minister that you would have given him or her if they had performed the ceremony. A fine-quality gift of a personal nature would be more appropriate for your uncle.

We are both the same denomination. Whose church do we marry in?

Traditionally, the marriage takes place in the bride's church. If for some reason that is a problem or source of contention, perhaps an alternative third site would be an acceptable compromise.

We're of different denominations. How do we choose which church to marry in?

Select the one you both feel most comfortable with. Or you may compromise with a nondenominational church or civil ceremony.

We're getting married in a religious denomination different from our families. They are unfamiliar with the service and keep asking me what they should do. What do I tell them?

The general rule is to follow the lead of the congregation. Stand, sit, sing, pray when everyone else does. If there is a part that they do not wish to participate in, they should sit quietly until that portion of the service is over. For example, Protestants in a Catholic church are not expected to genuflect, cross themselves, or kneel. You might also consider printing simple programs for your guests to guide them through the service.

It seems like every couple I know wrote their own wedding vows. Neither of us are talented at writing. Will our vows still be meaningful if we don't write our own?

Yes. Traditional written ceremonies have been meaningfully exchanged by millions of couples. It's the feelings behind the words, not the words themselves that are the essence of your ceremony.

Both of our families have varied religious backgrounds. We would like to combine these and a few other traditions in our ceremony. Is it acceptable to combine traditions from several different religions?

To avoid confusing your families, you may wish to have preprinted programs available so that they can understand, follow, and, if necessary, participate in your ritual. If some of your guests are strongly attached to a particular denomination they may be delighted that you included some of their customs, or they may be displeased. But the ceremony is for you, your fiancé, and your officiant to determine.

Why do we exchange wedding rings?

Since ancient times, it has been customary for the groom to present his bride with some sort of token during the wedding ceremony. In many cultures, the bride gives him a token in return. The ring, being an endless circle, is a symbol of continuity.

We hate the thought of crying children or restless toddlers destroying the solemnity of our ceremony. How can we politely ask people to keep their children home for the ceremony?

If you insist on this, parents will have the choice of either hiring a baby-sitter or staying home. Most parents of children who wouldn't be able to behave during a service will leave them home if they can. On the other hand, one of the purposes of marriage is joining two families, and children are a part of the families. A restless child or giggling toddler may not destroy your service; it may just make it more real, more human. However, if you can't abide the idea, then a handwritten note enclosed with the invitation explaining your reasons would be the best way to avoid offense. Be sure to mention that no children will be invited, otherwise they may feel you are singling out their little darlings!

How can we inform our guests they should not take photographs during the ceremony?

A sign in the vestibule, a note on the ceremony program, or a brief announcement from the head usher before the mothers of the bride and groom are seated would all be satisfactory options.

Must we have musicians at the ceremony?

Harmonious strains of soothing music in the air is customary prior to the beginning of the ceremony. The pomp of the wedding march and other musical selections help add to the distinctive observance taking place. If the sounds of music are distasteful to you, or if you feel it would somehow take away from the solemnity of the occasion, the decision to eliminate musical accompaniment is entirely yours.

What is a wedding program?

It's a guide to who is participating and what will take place during the wedding ceremony.

Why would I need a program?

They are especially helpful if you are having an interfaith or intercultural marriage, so that guests will understand all that is happening. Even for those familiar with your type of ceremony, printing the words to prayers and hymns will help guests follow and participate. They are also a souvenir if you have written your own vows. Last, they are a way of honoring and identifying ceremony participants.

What should a program look like?

Depending on your budget and the formality of the ceremony, it can be as simple as a single printed sheet to as elaborate as an engraved program. Many couples design a cover and program on their personal computers. If your ceremony site is especially attractive you might include a photo or sketch of it on your cover.

What information should I include in the program?

Here's an example of a fairly detailed program. You may increase or decrease the amount of information you wish to provide.

Front cover

Date

Time

Place

Full names of bride and groom

Inside page one

Officiant's name

Names of honor attendants

Names of other attendants, ushers, and so on

Names of soloists, musicians

Parents' names

Inside page two

Titles of readings and songs in the order they will occur

Words may follow titles if you wish

Any explanations of customs you feel will be helpful

Back cover

Your wedding vows

Thank you to guests, parents

Any special information about ceremony site

Information about or map for getting to reception site

Who pays for the programs?

The bride's family; programs are part of the wedding stationery.

How are the programs distributed?

Some couples have the ushers distribute them; others have a few friends stand at the door and hand them to each guest as they enter.

Picking Their Perches: Ceremony Seating

How does the usher seat the guests?

Ushers stand to the left of the inside door. As guests arrive, the usher asks if they are with the bride or groom and seats them accordingly. In Christian religious denominations, the bride's family is seated on the left, the groom's on the right. The opposite is true for Jewish weddings and some military weddings.

When an usher is seating a woman guest, she takes his arm. Any male accompanying her walks beside the usher. The usher leads the way to a vacant seat and then stands aside while the guest(s) step in. Some early arrivals ask to be seated in choice aisle seats. Unlike the etiquette for normal services, at a wedding they should be allowed to keep their seats on the aisle and not have to move over for new arrivals.

Does the usher take the arm of a male guest?

No. He offers his arm to a female guest but merely escorts a male guest. The only exception would be if the guest was quite elderly or having difficulty walking.

What if a female is already escorted by a male? Does the usher let the male with her do the seating?

No. If a female arrives with an escort, the usher still takes her arm and walks her to her seat. Her companion walks next to the usher.

What if two women arrive at the same time and there is only one usher? Whom does the usher seat first?

The usher should offer his arm to the elder. The other lady may either follow behind or wait for another usher to seat her.

Teenagers think of themselves as grown up, and we don't want to hurt any feelings. How old does someone have to be before they can be escorted to their seat?

Children under the age of fifteen usually follow their parents unescorted.

What does a head usher do at the ceremony?

He is responsible for coordinating the other ushers in seating the guests. He is aware of which guests should be seated in the honor or reserved section and relays this information to the other ushers.

My future mother-in-law has asked several times about seating people "in the ribbons." I'm too embarrassed to tell her that I have no idea what she is talking about. What does that mean?

It means seating in the honor section. Traditionally, the first few rows are reserved as honor seating for immediate family. The rows were marked with ribbons or bows. Thus the saying *in the ribbons*.

My family is much larger; won't the seating look out of balance? Does the bride/left–groom/right rule have to apply in a case like this?

A perfect balance isn't necessary, but in a situation where you know there will be a major imbalance you may have ushers seat guests to balance the sides. The only "rule" is that immediate family should still sit on their traditional side.

What should the ushers do after the bride's mother is seated?

The aisle carpet is laid and the outer church doors are closed. No one else is formally seated after the bride's mother. Late-arriving guests are asked to stand in the vestibule until the processional is over. They would then seat themselves in the back of the church.

Where are our grandparents seated?

Traditionally, your parents, brothers, and sisters sit in the first row behind the attendants. Grandparents and other close relatives sit in the row behind them. However, if you have a very small family there is no reason they cannot all sit together in the first row behind the attendants.

Where and when are the groom's parents seated?

They are seated in the aisle seats of the first row behind the attendants. If they are not taking part in the processional, the groom's mother is seated by the head usher about five minutes before the ceremony is to begin. The groom's father follows behind.

Where and when is the bride's mother seated?

She is seated by the head usher, in the aisle seat of the first row behind the attendants. If she is not part of the processional, she is seated just before the ceremony is about to begin.

Where and when is the bride's father seated?

After the bride's father escorts the bride in the processional, he joins the bride's mother in the first row after the attendants.

My parents are divorced but friendly. Neither has remarried. How are they seated?

They may sit together; there is no reason they shouldn't. Divorced parents are usually separated in seating arrangements due to animosity. If there is no animosity, lucky you!

My parents are divorced and each has remarried. My grandmother says my mother and father should sit together at the ceremony, and their new spouses would sit together in the next row. Is that right?

No. Your mother would sit on the aisle in the row behind the attendants with her current spouse. Your father would sit on the aisle with his current spouse in the row just behind your mother.

My mother left when I was young, and I was raised by my stepmother. Now my mother has come back into my life. Which one is treated as "mother" and sits in the first pew? Which one would my father sit with? Do they all sit in the same row?

If they get along, it would be wonderful for them all to sit in the same row. The problem with having a traditional wedding in a nontraditional world is there aren't always easy answers to questions like this. Talk to everyone involved and your clergyperson for suggestions. Each unique situation has its own answer. If you are totally at a loss for what to do, cite tradition. Traditionally, the mother of the bride is the woman who gave birth to you. No matter what her actions were later, that can't be taken away. If you are having a traditional wedding, your mother is the woman who would be seated as mother of the bride.

My sister and I may have a double wedding. How are two sets of groom's parents seated?

They may either share the first row or sit one row behind the other. As far as determining who sits in which row or who sits on the aisle seat if they share a row, they can decide the method. Flipping a coin, drawing straws, or any other problem-resolving game they can agree upon might be used.

My cousin and I are thinking of a double wedding. Suddenly, our mothers are arguing over who will sit on the aisle in the first row. How would we seat our parents?

First, are you sure that this is a good idea? You two may be close, but if your mothers are not it may be a difficult road ahead. Wedding decisions can be very emotional, and if they are disagreeing already there may be many problems and disagreements in the future.

If you decide to continue with the double wedding, they would either share the first row or one would sit in the row behind the other. If they share a row, the elder traditionally sits on the aisle. If they choose to sit one behind the other, they can either allow the elder the row in front or resolve it with a game of chance, such as flipping a coin.

If I spot an uninvited guest before the ceremony, what should I do?

Is your ceremony in a location with limited seating? Are you a celebrity, or is there some other reason you need to control access to the site? If so, then you would definitely ask the ushers to quietly escort them out. However, if they are sitting in the back quietly and not taking the space of an invited guest, you may just leave them there if you like.

What should the ushers do after the recessional?

They "bow out" each row of remaining guests, beginning in the front.

You Can't Roller-skate in a Buffalo Herd: Processional and Recessional

What is a processional?

A processional is the march of the wedding party into the ceremony site as the ceremony is about to begin. The *recessional* is their march out.

How do I know the proper order to line everyone up for the processional?

Actually, you shouldn't have to. Your ceremony officiant is well versed in the customary traditions for your type of wedding and in the pros and cons of any variations. You can discuss it with him or her ahead of time. This is the reason for a rehearsal before the wedding: so everyone knows where he or she will be on the big day.

How does the groom enter?

In Protestant, Catholic, and nondenominational ceremonies, the groom and his honor attendant enter at the front of the church, usually from a side sacristy door. They stand together and await the processional to march toward them.

In Jewish ceremonies, the customs may vary according to whether the ceremony is Orthodox, Conservative, or Reform.

How does the officiant enter?

Depending on custom, the formality of the wedding, and personal preference, the officiant either awaits the processional at the front of the church or marches at the head of the processional.

When and how do the groomsmen and bridesmaids enter?

In Protestant, Catholic, and nondenominational services the wedding party usually enters first in the processional, coming from the back of the church. An alternative is for them to enter with the groom and his honor attendant at the front of the church.

In some Jewish processionals, the groomsmen follow the groom's grandparents up the aisle.

Are the groomsmen supposed to enter alone or accompanied by bridesmaids?

Both traditions are popular. In very formal weddings they tend to enter in separate groups—bridesmaids, groomsmen. Otherwise, it's more a matter of personal preference and the particular religious tradition of your faith.

Must we have an equal number of bridesmaids and groomsmen?

No. If you have an extra groomsman or bridesmaid, he or she would walk in alone, ahead of the rest.

In what order should we place the attendants?

If they are entering in separate groups, they are usually paired by height, the shortest in front, tallest in back. If you have an uneven number, the shortest would walk in alone, ahead of the other pairs.

Must the bridesmaids enter in pairs?

If you have more than four, they usually enter in pairs. Otherwise they enter alone, one following the next.

How does the junior bridesmaid enter?

She would precede the honor attendant, which would place her after the bridesmaids.

What if there are two junior bridesmaids? Should they enter together?

They may enter individually or together.

Where does the honor attendant walk?

The honor attendant walks in front of the flower girl(s) and ring bearer(s). The flower girl and the ring bearer walk directly in front of the bride.

What if there are two honor attendants? May they walk up the aisle together?

Yes. Or you can have them in a single file, with the elder first.

Does the ring bearer walk before or after the flower girl?

He may either walk next to the flower girl or walk alone in front of the flower girl.

May both of my parents be in the processional?

Yes. It is a nice alternative.

May the groom's parents be in the processional?

Traditionally the grooms' parents do march in the Jewish processional. For the most part, it's up to the couple and the officiant. If the couple wishes for their parents to be in the processional, there's no reason why they shouldn't be.

May I have my father and stepfather escort me together?

It's the bride's father's privilege to "give" his daughter away. If such an action would not deeply hurt your father, there's no reason why they shouldn't.

May I ask my grandfather or brother to give me away?

If your father is deceased or if for some reason he is unable to attend the ceremony, you may select any relative for the honor. Whom are you closest to? Who would appreciate the honor the most? That would be the one to choose.

If there are two center aisles, which do we use?

You may either close one of them off or use one (the left) for the processional and the other (right) for the recessional.

May the groom and I walk up the aisle together?

Yes. If the wedding is very informal or if you are significantly older, many couples follow this custom.

I was married before; should I walk alone?

You may if you like, or you may still have your father escort you. In some cases, especially among older couples, the bride and groom walk up the aisle together.

Must we have a processional?

In all but the smallest weddings they are just a tradition. In very small ceremonies, the couple usually just stands before the officiant. The honor attendants and guests stand around them.

What is the traditional order for the processional?

Christian

Groomsmen

Bridesmaids

Honor attendant

Ring bearer

Flower girl

Bride and her father

Jewish

Cantor

Rabbi

Bride's grandparents

Groom's grandparents

Groomsmen

Best man

Groom's father, groom, groom's mother

Bridesmaids

Honor Attendant

Ring Bearer

Flower Girl

Bride's father, bride, bride's mother

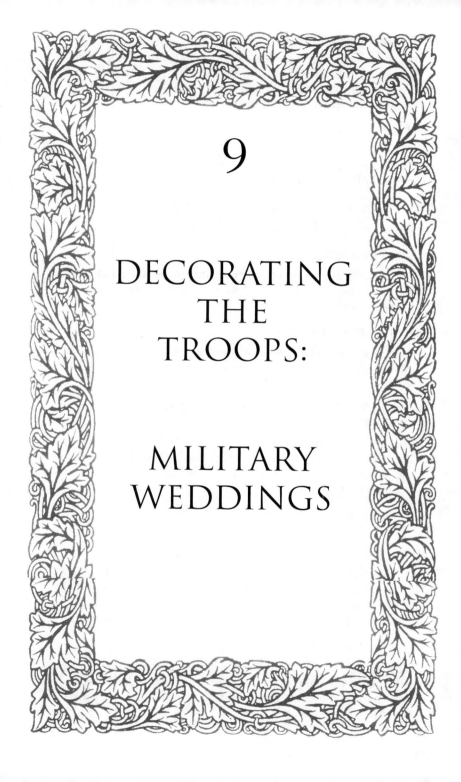

9

DECORATING
THE
TROOPS:

MILITARY
WEDDINGS

What is a military wedding?

Local protocol varies, so check with your commanding officer. In general, it is for commissioned officer(s) who marry in dress uniform. An American flag and the standards of your military unit(s) are displayed during the ceremony.

What is the "arch of swords"?

After the recessional, you and the groom pass through an arch of swords or sabers. The arch is formed by those of your ushers who are officers in full uniform.

What if some of my ushers are not in the military?

These ushers would stand at attention in the line.

How is seating different?

Rank is carefully observed when seating guests. Generals would be in the front, followed by sergeants, privates behind the sergeants, and recruits in the back.

Is the bride still on the left side?

Yes. If the male officer wears a sword or saber, the bride and her attendants stand on the right (since swords are worn on the left side).

My sister's fiancé is a captain in the Naval Reserve. May a reserve officer have a military wedding?

Yes. Any officer on active duty in either regular or reserve forces may have a military wedding. According to most local protocols, the designation *Reserve* would appear on the invitation after his branch of service:

Lieutenant Colonel Daniel Robert Pielow
United States Naval Reserve

What sort of military wedding may an enlisted person have?

An enlisted person may marry in uniform, but the rest of the celebration would follow civilian traditions. Traditionally, if the bride is the enlisted person, she would wear a bridal gown. However, the bride may also wear her uniform if she wishes.

How would titles be noted on the invitations?

The title appears on the same line before the name if the person is on active duty and ranked captain or above in the Army or lieutenant senior grade or above in the Navy. For lower ranks, the title is listed after the name.

Higher ranks:

Major Sarah Elizabeth Sims
United States Army

Lower ranks:

Michael Wayne Grace
Ensign, United States Navy

Do we cut the cake differently?

Yes. The groom cuts the cake with his sword or saber.

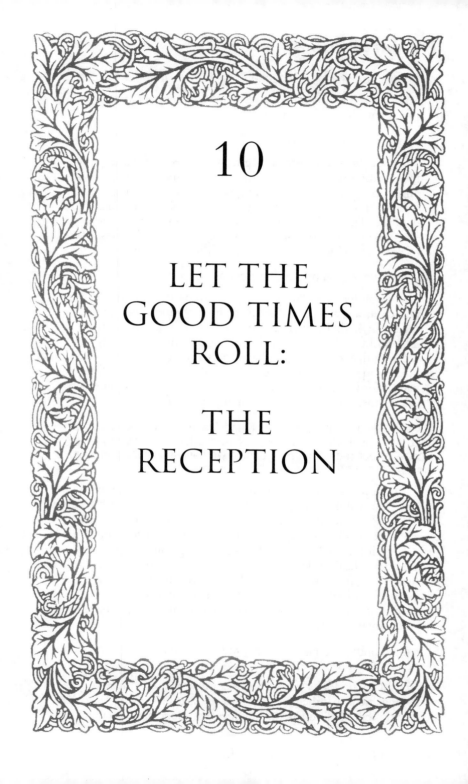

10

LET THE GOOD TIMES ROLL:

THE RECEPTION

Pre-Party Primer

What if we do not have a reception? What do we do after the ceremony?

After the recessional, form a receiving line to greet your guests and thank them for coming.

What occurs at the reception?

Traditionally, the reception begins with a receiving line, in which the wedding party welcomes the guests. A meal or dessert and punch are served. Toasts are proposed to the new couple. After socializing with guests for a while, the couple ceremonially cuts the cake. The bride tosses her bouquet to nonmarried females. The groom tosses the bride's garter to nonmarried males. Many receptions include dancing and musical entertainment.

May we have a cash bar for the alcoholic beverages?

No, absolutely not. You invite guests to participate in your joy and celebrate with you. As part of the invitation, you provide a repast—whether it is cake and punch or a three-course meal. The tradition has continued since ancient times. It's only recently that some couples have had the audacity to expect their guests to pay for something at the wedding reception. If you can't afford it, don't offer it. Please do not insult your guests by asking them to pay for any item at your party.

My uncle tends to drink too much and create scenes. My mother becomes upset when I suggest not inviting him. We want to serve alcohol at our reception. How should we handle a relative that has a drinking problem?

It's hard to leave a close relative out of such a celebration. Such a decision will inevitably result in hurt feelings and possible family feuds. Realistically, just talking to someone will not guarantee good behavior. Although, if you or your mother feel comfortable trying, it may help. If you do, avoid being confrontational. Just state your fears and the reasons behind them. Ask him to make a special effort to avoid a scene. If you have someone who has a positive outlook, knows your uncle, and could have some influence on him, you might ask the person to keep an eye on your uncle for the evening.

I love the bridal bouquet I'm going to have; I don't want to throw my bouquet. Is that OK?

Yes. Many brides have their florist create a smaller, simpler arrangement that they toss to the assemblage before they leave. You can do that or eliminate the bouquet toss altogether if you prefer.

I don't plan to wear a garter. But my bridesmaids insist I must have one to toss to a crowd of single men at the reception. I don't want anything to do with that meaningless tradition. Is it a necessary part of a big wedding reception?

No. This custom is a throwback to medieval times and has no special meaning in today's celebrations. Like many of the practices at weddings today, it should be followed only if you wish to utilize it. If you feel uncomfortable, don't do it.

Are we required to have music?

Some sort of musical accompaniment adds to the festivities no matter what your wedding style. The more formal and elaborate the wedding is, the more music you would have. Music is expected but not required.

How do we decide what kind of music to have?

It depends partly on the style of reception you are having, and partly on your budget and personal taste. Where at a small, informal reception classical music playing in the background from a CD is fine; at a very large, very formal reception you would probably have a live band with a disc jockey backup and a pianist, violinist, or flutist playing softly during the meal. Most weddings fall somewhere between the two.

We eloped to Hawaii last month; now my parents are planning a belated reception for this summer. How does this work? Do I still wear my wedding gown?

The reception, with all its decorations and traditions, would take place as if you were married on that day. You should wear your wedding gown so that everyone can see and enjoy it!

I'm from Colorado and my husband is from New Hampshire. His family is planning a second reception for us when we visit their area. Would we wear our wedding clothes? How is this usually done?

Some families hold a belated reception, complete with formalwear, elaborate decorations, cake, food, and music. Others offer a variety of simpler formats, down to an informal meet-the-new-bride-and-groom gathering. Whether you should wear formalwear would depend on the type of occasion. If they are planning a formal party, you might compromise by asking your mother to ship your dress to their home just after the wedding so it will be there waiting for your arrival.

Stand by Your Man and Mom and Dad and ... The Receiving Line

What is the point of a receiving line?

The reception begins with you greeting your guests as a way to make them feel welcome. It is formed just inside the entrance of the reception site. You will be busy and distracted most of the evening, so this is a good way to ensure you are able to see all of your guests at least once.

What should I say to people as they pass through the line?

The mothers (or hostesses) greet the guests initially and introduce them to each other. Then you and the groom do the same. If you don't know who the person is, smile and ask. Thank each guest for coming but save lengthy discussions for later.

In what order is everyone supposed to stand in the receiving line?

The bride's mother (or reception hostess) stands directly inside the door. Next is the groom's mother, then the bride, groom, bride's honor attendant, groom's honor attendant, bridesmaids, and groomsmen.

Is it necessary for the bridesmaids and groomsmen to stand in the receiving line?

No. The bride and groom make that decision. Many times they are family members and it's a chance for them to greet everyone, too.

Do our fathers stand in the receiving line?

Traditionally, no. But if they do, the groom's father stands just after the bride's mother.

Should children in the wedding party stand in line?

No. Children in the wedding party do not stand in the receiving line.

Planned Seating Is Stress-relieving

Why does the wedding party sit at a head table facing everyone?

It's a customary form that allows it to seem like they are at everyone else's table.

How do I arrange the wedding party at the head table?

The bride and the groom are at the center with the honor attendants flanking them. Bridesmaids, groomsmen, and ushers would also be seated there. They are seated in a male/female/male/female pattern.

Do children in the wedding party sit at the head table?

Children who are in the wedding party are seldom seated at the head table, unless they are older and well-behaved.

Where are our parents seated?

If there is room, parents of the bride and groom may be seated at the head table. If not, they are seated at an honor table.

Neither set of parents wants to sit at the head table. Where are our parents seated?

A separate honor table is usually used to include parents, grandparents, officiant, siblings, and others very close to the couple.

How do we indicate who sits where?

Fewer weddings these days have place cards for guest dinner seating. But they are still practical for honor seating. Use place cards in those locations to avoid confusion and embarrassment.

My parents are divorced. May I have two honor tables so they won't have to sit together?

In this case it would be a good idea. There is nothing wrong with having more than one honor table. If you both have large families, it will be a necessity.

I want to have place cards at each dinner setting. How do I determine the seating arrangements?

Alternate men and women in every other chair. Keep those who don't get along separate. Try not to put anyone at a table made up entirely of strangers. Avoid seating elderly people too close to the musicians.

Combine groupings so that everyone has an opportunity to meet someone new. Be conscious that those who have traveled long distances will be looking forward to visiting their friends and relatives.

I'm picturing mass confusion as three hundred guests try to find their place cards. What can I do to help guests find their proper seats?

Number the tables and have the caterer put place cards at each setting. Place a large seating chart near the guest book that lists everyone's names alphabetically and their table numbers.

Where should I seat spouses of members of the wedding party?

They are usually seated dispersed among the rest of the guests.

Speak Easy: Toasts

What should one say when toasting someone?

A toast is best kept short, simple, and sincere. It should sound straight from the heart. The person making the toast should speak clearly and loud enough so all can hear. The toaster refers to the person being toasted and says something nice about him or her. When the toast is finished, the toaster raises his or her glass so people know the toast is finished.

How do you toast?

When the verbal tribute is finished, neighbors clink their glasses and sip.

When does the toasting begin?

At smaller gatherings or cocktail receptions, the toasting begins after the receiving line breaks up. At a dinner reception, it follows the blessing and precedes the meal.

Who offers the toast at the engagement party?

The bride's father, wishing the couple a lifetime of happiness together.

Who offers the toast at the bachelor party?

The best man toasts the groom. The groom toasts his bride, even though she isn't present.

Who offers the toast at the rehearsal dinner?

The groom's father begins and the best man follows. Usually everyone in the wedding party offers a toast to the happy couple.

Who offers the toast at the reception?

The best man toasts the happy couple. The groom toasts his bride. Today, many brides now toast their grooms in return.

What do I do when I am being toasted?

When you are being toasted, you do not sip or raise your glass. You acknowledge the honor by nodding and smiling at the person offering the toast to you.

There will be some at our reception who do not drink. We don't want them to feel uncomfortable during the toasts. What is a nonalcoholic substitute to toast with?

Have your servers offer each guest the option of nonalcoholic beverages such as sparkling water or apple juice.

My fiancé's mother died last year, and he wants to include a toast to her at the reception. My mother says it is not the time or place to do that. I want to respect his mother's memory, but I don't want to cast a pall of gloom over the reception. Should I allow my fiancé to toast his deceased mother at the reception?

It's wonderful that your fiancé wants to honor his mother. However, a wedding is a celebration among the living—and not the time or place to remember the deceased.

The Final Feast: The Reception Meal

If my ceremony occurs at 10 A.M., would I serve a wedding breakfast?

A breakfast gathering would be a fine celebration, with wedding cake and champagne for dessert. It is, after all, a very special occasion!

What's the difference between a wedding lunch and a wedding tea?

Lunch takes place between 12 noon and 2 P.M. A tea takes place between 2 and 5 P.M. A lunch might include a meal with cocktails. A tea would be hors d'oeuvres, and coffee, tea, or punch. The highlight of the gathering is the cutting of the cake.

We've been told a cocktail reception is more cost-effective. What exactly is it?

It is more cost-effective because you would not be paying for a meal or for musicians. These celebrations usually start between 4 and 6 P.M. As with a tea reception, you serve hors d'oeuvres and beverages. However, in a cocktail reception alcoholic beverages are also included. The cake cutting is the height of the celebration.

What will my guests expect at a dinner reception?

It will begin between 6 and 8 P.M., and a cocktail hour may precede the dinner. Whether it's sit-down or buffet style, guests are served a full meal. Alcoholic beverages are available (unless it violates strong personal beliefs). The cake is cut and served after dinner. There is usually music and dancing as part of the celebration.

If most of our guests aren't religious, should we say grace?

This depends on what kind of marriage ceremony you will be having. If it will be a religious ceremony, it is customary to have a prayer before your meal. However, if religious beliefs are somehow an issue among your families, you have the option of asking for a moment of silent reflection and thanksgiving before the meal begins. If it is a civil ceremony and you and your husband are not religious, any prayers would be entirely at your discretion.

Who says grace?

If your officiant will be present, it is customary to ask him or her to offer a prayer. Otherwise, the best man, your honor attendant, friend, or anyone you choose may do it. However, prepare whomever you choose ahead of time. Don't spring it on him or her five minutes before the meal will begin.

How do we say grace?

The prayer is said before the meal is begun. The person saying the prayer advises the gathering to stand or sit, hold hands or fold hands, and usually to bow their heads.

Among the most common are the following:

Christian:

Bless us, O Lord, and these gifts which we are about to receive from Thy bounty, through Christ our Lord, Amen.

Jewish:

Blessed are you, Lord God of all creation. Through your goodness we have this meal to offer, which earth has given and human hands have made.

We're at a loss about how to plan a wedding meal. So many people are on special diets. How do I plan a meal?

Plan a variety of selections so that all can pick and choose enough to satisfy themselves. The vegetarian can enjoy salads and other dishes. Those on special diets should be well-practiced in finding a few items they can enjoy. People with very particular restrictions will probably eat their own meal before they arrive. Just place a few items on their plate in order to be social.

If our meal is served buffet style, may I still have the wedding party served seated? My new husband thinks that would be rude. Would it?

No, it would be very unusual to see the bride and groom standing in line with their plates. They and the wedding party are traditionally served seated. Your guests will expect it to be that way.

I do not care for sweets. Must I have a wedding cake?

How does your new husband feel? A wedding cake is very traditional, and your guests will be expecting one. Why disappoint them?

Must I have a stodgy white wedding cake with boring white frosting?

Only if you have a very formal wedding. Many brides now choose different flavors, sometimes having each tier a different flavor. Often, the frosting matches the color of the bridal party attire.

When do we cut the cake?

If the cake will be served as dessert, after dinner. If not, arrange to do it shortly before you leave the gathering.

What is a groom's cake?

This is a dessert for the guests to take home. It is cut by the caterers and put in decorative white boxes with the new couple's initials and wedding date. Each departing guest takes a box. In some regions, this is traditionally a fruitcake. In others, it is a chocolate cake.

You Put Your Left Foot in and Shake it All About: Dancing

Is there a special order to the dancing?

Typically, dancing begins with the bride and groom dancing slowly to a meaningful romantic song. After a few minutes, it is customary for the bride's father to cut in, and then the groom dances with the bride's mother. Then the groom's father dances with the bride and the groom dances with his mother. The honor attendants and then all the wedding party begin dancing. Then the guests join the dancing.

We don't know how to slow dance; what should we do?

That first dance together is a very strong observance. It will be hard to ignore or disregard the custom. You may find yourselves being prodded and teased if you try to leave it out. Practice waltzing now. If you aren't able to practice, the time-honored alternative is to just hold each other and sway back and forth a little bit.

How do we select music that people of all ages can enjoy?

It's good that you are concerned about entertaining all of your guests. Talk to your musicians or disc jockey. They'll be experienced in helping you to select the songs that will receive the best responses on the dance floor. Another option is to ask people of different age groups the names of their favorite tunes. Each decade has plenty of melodies with a good beat that will inspire listeners to move their feet.

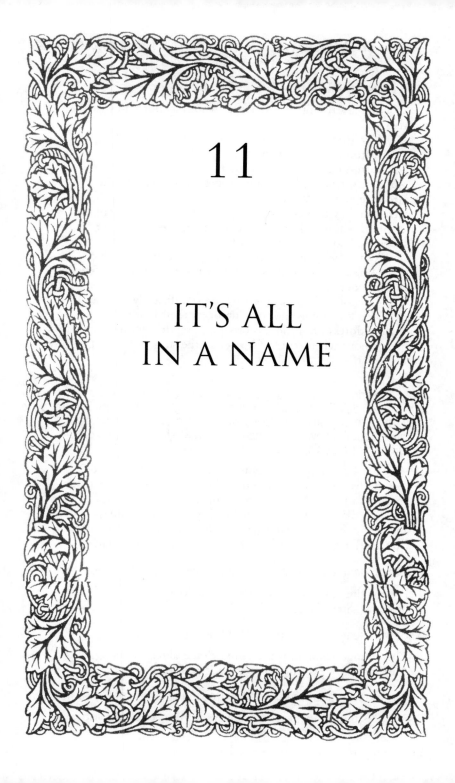

11

IT'S ALL
IN A NAME

Words to Merge the Connections: Introductions

Ten Tips about Introductions:

1) You always introduce people who may not know each other.

2) Introduce less important to more important.

3) Introduce younger to older.

4) Introduce a man to a woman.

5) You introduce by saying, "Guest A, I would like to introduce you to Guest B."

6) You may also introduce by first saying the name of the person to whom the other is being introduced. For example, "Guest A, may I present Guest B."

7) When being introduced, nod or smile and say hello.

8) When you are introduced, repeat the name back to help you to remember it.

9) Do not address people who are significantly older or of higher rank as a governor or senator by their first names.

10) Address professionals providing services by their last names, not their first: Dr. Grovsener, the surgeon; Mrs. Peabody, the florist.

I was shopping with my maid of honor and saw one of my distant great aunts. I couldn't think of her name even though I had just mailed her an invitation. I'm embarrassed to admit that I hid behind a rack of clothes because I didn't know how to handle it. What should I do if I can't remember a person's name?

Here are a few responses: "Auntie, have you met Jane Doe?" Hopefully, your aunt would offer her name when she extends her hand to Jane. Or, "I'm sorry auntie, my mind is full of wedding plans and I can't think of my own name today or yours. This is my maid of honor, Jane Doe." Hopefully, your aunt would offer her name when she extends her hand to Jane.

Who is presented to whom when I introduce a man and a woman?

Present the man to the woman: "Mrs. MacKenzie, this is my husband, Steve Deroshia."

Who is presented to whom when I introduce two women?

The younger woman is presented to the older woman: "Aunt Amelia, may I present my friend Crystal."

Who is presented to whom when I introduce two men of the same age?

The less important person is always introduced to the more

important person: "Governor Gannon, I'd like you to meet Richard Linn."

What exception is made when introducing family members?

No matter how prominent your family members are, the nonfamily person's name comes first. For example: "Mr. Gustafson, may I present my sister, Dr. Melanie Stevens?"

What are some friendly ways to introduce people?

Some forms include, "David Johannsen, *I'd like you to meet* Michael Bernard." "Mrs. Currothers, *this is my friend,* Roberta Rusch." "Dr. Sanders, *have you met my husband,* Joseph Cavenaugh?"

Should I use first and last names when I introduce people?

Yes, unless the last name is obvious, such as when introducing a sibling who has the same last name as yours.

How do we introduce my own parents to his?

Traditionally, the groom's parents contact the bride's parents and the two sets of parents get together (or correspond) on their own. If for some reason that would be awkward, there's no reason you both can't join the parents. If the groom's parents don't take the first step, the bride's parents should. It should all be very friendly, not a "they must follow the traditional rules" type of thing.

How would my mother introduce my husband's parents?

"May I present my son-in-law's parents, Mr. and Mrs. Gabriel?" or "I'd like you to meet John's parents, Mr. and Mrs. Gabriel."

My parents are divorced and I hardly see my mother. How do we introduce both sets of parents when there is a divorce involved?

Whichever parent you are closest to would be most likely to contact his parents.

My husband's parents are divorced. I understand that his parents are supposed to contact mine, but how does it work when his parents don't speak to each other?

Your parents would contact his parents separately.

How do I introduce my different family members?

Stepmother:

Despite all the bad press, there is nothing wrong with being a stepparent. Say "This is my stepmother, Cathy Jones."

Stepchild:

"This is my stepson, John Jones."

Sister-in-law:

"This is Kelly, my brother Jeff's wife" or "This is Kelly, Jeff's wife."

Widowed sister-in-law (my brother is deceased):

If it's a casual introduction, meaning that your former sister-in-law and the person probably won't meet again, it is not necessary to explain the relationship. Just introduce her as you would any friend. If the introduction is more formal, you may explain: "I'd like you to meet Elizabeth Denton. She's (my brother's) (John's) widow." If she has remarried you might say, "This is Elizabeth Silverman. She is my brother John's widow, and she is now married to Dr. Silverman."

Former sister-in-law (she and my brother are divorced):

"I would like you to meet Caroline Schumacker. She was Christopher's wife and is now married to Zachary Schumacker."

Former mother-in-law (I am divorced from her son):

"This is Mrs. Calloway. She is Cara's grandmother." Or, "This is Mrs. Calloway, my first husband's mother."

Brother's live-in girlfriend:

If it's a formal introduction, you do not need to explain their relationship. Just introduce her. Informally, you might introduce her and add, "She is the wonderful woman who lives with my brother Alexander."

What a Difference a Name Makes: Titles

What is the difference between Miss, Mrs., and Ms.?

The first two have always been tied to marital status. "Miss Lane" is an unmarried woman. "Mrs. Lane" is a married woman. "Ms. Lane" is a social title, indicating that the person is female, but not connected to marital status.

What do I call my husband's parents?

This is a very personal choice; ideally your in-laws should indicate their preference. Mr. or Mrs. is cold and rather formal. Consider using a different form of *mother* or *father* than you use for own parents—*Mom, dad, papa, mama.* Your in-laws might request that you use their first names. Another alternative is to use their last name initial, such as Mr. & Mrs. B.

What do I call my new husband's other relatives, such as his aunts and uncles?

You refer to them the same way that your spouse does: "Uncle Joe," "Aunt Jane." If you are formally introducing them, you would say something like "Senator Brownstone, this is David's uncle, Maxwell Ollesini."

My honor attendant is a widow. Is she a *maid* or *matron* of honor?

She's your honor attendant or matron of honor.

Must I take my husband's name?

No, not usually. Except in rare instances, it is a cultural tradition, not a legal one.

I worked very hard for my degree and have established myself as a general practitioner. I want to keep my professional name, but my husband is upset. Can you suggest an alternative?

You might keep your maiden name for professional use, going by the name: "Dr. Pauline Anderson," and use your new husband's name socially, "Dr. Pauline Hutchinson and Mr. Jeremy Hutchinson."

My first husband is deceased. What should my two children call their stepfather?

It's best to let the children decide. Do not force a version of *dad* or *daddy* on them. If they do not want to use a variation of the title *father*, a nickname or his first name is also acceptable.

I am going to be a stepmother. My stepdaughter's mother is still alive. What should the child call me?

If her mother is still living, try to help her to select a variation of *mother* that she does not use with her living parent. A nickname or your first name is also acceptable.

How do I inform people that I have kept my maiden name?

Enclose a card with your wedding invitations or announcements. It may say "Rebecca Burdette will retain her maiden name for all legal and social purposes after the marriage."

I don't like the way our names sound when they are hyphenated; however, I want to keep my name, too. What are alternatives to hyphenating our names?

You might use your maiden name as your middle name. Or, each of you can keep your own name.

If we hyphenate, how do we decide which order to put the names in?

Most couples choose the order that sounds the best.

If we hyphenate our names, do we both use the hyphenated name?

Yes. If you hyphenate, you should both use the hyphenated format.

I'm trying to decide about keeping my maiden name or hyphenating. I really don't want to give up my name. But I want children, and I'm not sure what their last name will be if I don't take my husband's name. If I don't take his name, what name will our children have?

If you keep your maiden name, your children can take either name—although traditionally they have the husband's name. If you hyphenate, children can be hyphenated, too. Or some parents choose to give the wife's maiden name to the children as a middle name. With so many alternative name choices and repeat marriages, many children travel through life with a different last name than their mothers.

How do I sign notes for wedding gifts received before the marriage?

Sign your maiden name to any thank-you letter written before the wedding. Sign your married or social name on those notes written after the marriage takes place.

12

WILL
YOU
RECEIVE?

When Presents Rain, They Pour Just Rewards: Showers

Who is supposed to give the wedding shower?

Traditionally, the shower is given by the maid of honor with assistance from the other female attendants. Members of the groom's family, coworkers, and other friends might also sponsor additional showers.

Every etiquette book says that a shower may not be given by a family member. What if all of my close friends are family members? Does this mean that I may not have a shower?

No, this is an exceptional situation. The idea behind the tradition is that the bride's family shouldn't look as though they are soliciting gifts. If her friends give the bride a shower it is supposed to seem less calculating.

I've been told that the maid of honor sponsors the wedding shower. I've also been told that immediate family members do not sponsor showers. What if my sister is my maid of honor?

She is sponsoring the shower as your maid of honor, not as your sister.

My maid of honor plans to give me a shower. When is the shower held?

Showers are usually held one to two months before the wedding date. The last few weeks before the wedding are much too hectic for parties.

My friends have said that they are giving me a shower, but no one has asked me for a guest list. Should I offer one?

Unless it is a surprise party, the bride or her mother usually provides a list of guests, upon request. You might discreetly check with your mom first. If she hasn't been asked for a list and the wedding is less than two months away, it wouldn't be improper for her to contact your honor attendant and ask about any shower plans.

I'm having several bridal showers. Is it OK to ask the same people to more than one?

Only your maid of honor, attendants, and immediate family (mother, grandmothers, siblings) should be invited to every shower.

If I've been married before may I still have a shower?

How long has it been since your first wedding? If it has been at least three years, a simple, low-key shower would not be considered improper. Rather than suggesting the more traditional shower gifts, a theme shower for a particular interest of yours would be more appropriate.

Should my registry information be included with the invitations?

A gift is supposed to be offered freely, and suggesting a gift to buy is considered poor manners. However, many guests today expect ideas about what to purchase so as not to choose something unsuitable. Good manners require that you not offer such a list unless it is specifically requested. At that time you may also make note of the shop(s) where you are registered.

My attendants say my fiancé is supposed to be at the shower. My fiancé says he doesn't want to be there. Should my fiancé attend the shower?

Traditionally, only the bride attends the shower. However, many men attend their wedding showers for two reasons: The gifts are now given to the bride and groom, and in many instances this will be the first time many family members will meet him. However, if he absolutely refuses to attend, no one should be offended.

What is a "Jack and Jill shower"?

These are multigender parties. The groom isn't the only male present and most female attendees bring dates. Gifts are given to the couple. The customary shower format of party games and favors is seldom used. After the gifts are opened, it tends to carry on like any other party.

Perks and Benefits: Gifts

Am I supposed to give my fiancé a gift when he presents me my engagement ring?

It is not a widespread tradition, but some women choose to give their fiancé a gift at the same time. The gift is usually a simple item of jewelry, such as cuff links, a watch, or a key chain.

Will I receive a gift in response to every invitation that I send?

Gift giving is an important part of our culture, and giving a wedding gift is a deeply held tradition. Some couples have tried to take advantage of this by sending invitations to people that they barely know. This will not work. You do not invite people to your wedding for their gift. You invite them for their company. Out of their joy in your happiness, they give you a gift. If they don't know you very well, they won't buy you a present.

If I was married before will I still receive gifts at this wedding?

No one is obligated to provide a gift at a second wedding. Your immediate family and very close friends will probably present you with gifts. As far as the other guests, most will give something. But their gifts will probably be less elaborate than the gifts you received for your first wedding.

We need to register for our wedding gifts. What type of gifts should I register for?

Generally, you register for items that will help you furnish your new home. Most couples focus on kitchen and dining room items and decorative items they will enjoy. This can include anything from cookware to monogrammed glassware, from framed oil paintings to a set of lamps. Guests try to choose items within their budget that will be a memento of the occasion.

I was married before, but my fiancé was not. Should we still register for gifts?

Traditionally, it is assumed that the female received most of the household items in any divorce. In second marriages, most couples register on a theme, perhaps for camping or sports equipment for a favorite shared hobby or for garden supplies for their new home.

My fiancé is divorced, but I have never been married. Should we still register for gifts?

Yes. Since household items are still considered the domain of the bride, this is your opportunity to select your preferences for your new home.

We don't need basic household items. What should we suggest when people ask about possible gifts?

Ask for things you would not usually buy for yourselves and might enjoy. Some ideas include a selection of gourmet foods such as imported cheeses, coffee, and tea or a fine bottle of wine or champagne; a tree or shrub for your garden; or something that adds to a hobby or collection you enjoy.

If we elope will we still receive gifts?

No one has an obligation to send a gift in this case. Some people will give you a gift anyway if they are especially close.

Traditionally, however, couples who elope do not receive wedding gifts.

Am I supposed to give a gift to each of my attendants?

Yes. Shortly before the wedding each attendant should receive a gift. Traditionally, these are given at the rehearsal dinner. Gifts are usually some permanent, personal memento of the occasion. Typically, the gift is a monogrammed piece of jewelry, a picture frame, or perhaps a special item handmade by you.

The groom also presents his attendants with gifts. Customarily, the gifts are items such as key rings, engraved pens, belt buckles, or money clips. In both cases, gifts to the honor attendants are slightly nicer than gifts that other attendants receive.

Are we required to give each guest a gift in the form of "favors" such as candies or scrolls with our names and wedding date inscribed?

No, favors are just a friendly way to offer each person who joined your celebration a memento of the occasion. But, they don't have to be expensive, and it might be fun to see how many still have their favors on your fiftieth wedding anniversary.

Are monetary gifts considered rude?

No. In some communities and ethnic cultures it is a tradition to give money as a gift. If it is customary in your family, then there is nothing wrong with it.

We are paying for our own wedding and hope to receive a certain amount of cash from each guest to cover our expenses. Since most people don't know how expensive a wedding can be, would it be wrong to mention a minimum cash amount for our gifts?

Absolutely. The amount of a gift—whether it is a purchased item or cash—should have nothing to do with the cost of the wedding, the size or elaborateness of the wedding, or the fact that the couple might have trouble paying for the wedding. The amount a guest spends on a gift should be based on the closeness and affection the guest has for the bride and groom and his or her financial capabilities.

My fiancé wants to display our gifts at the reception. My mother says that is not the right location to display them. May we display gifts at the reception?

Traditionally, gifts are displayed at the bride's parents' home before the wedding. This custom is seldom practiced anymore. It is rare, primarily for security reasons, to display the gifts at the reception site. However, if you do display gifts, you should hire a security guard.

How do we note monetary gifts if we display our presents?

You may use a list or individual cards that say: "Check from Mr. and Mrs. Del Giorno" or "Monetary gift from George Whitley."

How are gifts displayed?

Display the gifts on tables covered with simple cloths. Place each in an attractive position, with items of similar quality together—an item's inexpensiveness will be glaring if it's among expensive items. Some people separate the gifts by type—china, glassware, or silverware—or by color, pattern, shapes, or textures. Duplicates should be scattered as far apart as possible.

Is it OK to return a gift?

In general, no. Duplicate gifts may be exchanged. If the gift arrives broken, find out from where it was sent. If it came directly from the store, notify the store. If the gift giver sent it and the package was insured, notify the gift giver so he or she may place a claim. Otherwise, you should not return the gift unless the giver tells you that it would be acceptable. You are not supposed to ask; the gift giver is supposed to offer.

A mutual friend offered to take the wedding photographs as his gift to us. We know he can't afford much, but we prefer to hire a professional photographer. What should we do?

Explain that you'll look forward to his gift of providing a personal perspective of the day but that you have also hired a professional photographer to cover the wedding. After all, you want this good friend to be able to join in the celebration, too.

Gratitude Attitude: Saying Thanks

As I understand it, the main reason for sending a thank-you note is to acknowledge receipt of a gift. May I send a preprinted card stating that a gift has been received?

Don't you expect your guests to send you more than a wedding card? People who give you gifts have selected, bought, and wrapped a gift or shared a portion of their budget if they gave a monetary gift. In addition, the gift givers will have taken time to attend the wedding and reception and perhaps have spent money on clothing, travel, or a baby-sitter. They made an effort to celebrate with you. Taking a little of your own time to write a personal note in return is not just good manners, it is the least you could do in return.

How are acknowledgment cards worded?

Acknowledgment cards are printed cards that read some

variation of the following: Mr. and Mrs. Tiberius Caeser gratefully acknowledge the receipt of your wedding gift and offer their sincere thanks.

Acknowledgment cards do not replace thank-you notes. Their purpose is to buy time and acknowledge the receipt of a gift. You are still expected to send a personal thank-you note as soon as possible after the honeymoon.

When am I obligated to send a thank-you note?

For any party where you are a guest of honor, send a note to everyone who gave or helped with the party. You must also send a note for every wedding gift, even if you have thanked the gift giver in person.

May I send a thank-you note for a wedding gift before the wedding?

Yes. Ideally, you'll send out your notes as soon as each gift is received. That way you won't have a large pile to write after the honeymoon.

If I send a note before the wedding do I sign my maiden name or married name?

Sign all notes before the wedding with your maiden name and after the wedding with your married name.

Should we sign both of our names to the thank-you note?

Yes. The custom of only the bride's signing is very formal and traditional. Most couples sign their notes with both names nowadays.

How long do I have after the wedding to send out the thank-you notes?

Send the notes as soon as possible, ideally within one month of your wedding date. Even if you had a very large wedding, they should still be completed and mailed within three months after the wedding.

What information should be included in the thank-you note?

Refer to the gift and how it will be used. Then you must say something to show that you appreciate the time and money used to acquire it.

Whom do I address the note to?

Traditionally, the wife sends a gift to the bride. The bride writes a note thanking the wife. The husband is mentioned in the text of the note. Today, most gifts are sent to the bride and groom and signed by the husband and wife. In those cases, you can address the note to the husband and wife.

Traditional Thank-You Note:

> *Dear Diane:*
> *Al and I really appreciate the wonderful cookware*
> *set you and Steve gave us on our wedding day. We*
> *really needed a new set of frying pans. The lovely blue*
> *enamel color you chose complements our kitchen*
> *perfectly. We would love to have you and Steve over for*
> *dinner and I will contact you soon.*
> *Once again, thank you for your generosity.*
> *Sincerely,*
> *Francine*

How do I thank someone for a bizarre gift?

Such an item would be *distinctive, charming, unique,* or *stunning*—you might refer to "the distinctive blue clay pot" or "the stunning white ceramic figure." Tell the gift giver it will undoubtedly be in a special place in your new home.

I have received a few gifts that just don't fit in with my home. Is it OK to return a gift I don't like? Should I ask the gift giver for a receipt?

Unless the gift giver offers a receipt or suggests that it would be fine for you to return the gift, you should not return the gift.

We have received a few group gifts; one is from four people and the other is from seven people. Do I write individual thank-you notes for group gifts?

It depends on how the gift was presented. For a large group gift from coworkers, a handwritten note to all on the office bulletin board and an individual "Thank you" when you see the person will be sufficient. If each person in the group wrapped a portion (a place setting, for example) and signed that portion, then each should receive a thank-you note.

When we receive a monetary gift, are we supposed to mention the amount in the note?

Yes. It's also nice to add a description of how the money will be used.

It would be fast and easy to set up a basic thank-you note in my computer and adapt each for the individual's gift. I even have a font that looks like handwriting. Is there anything wrong with computer-

generated thank-you notes?

Yes, because you are supposed to take some time to write a personal note by hand, just as the gift giver took time to purchase a gift for you.

May I E-mail my thank-you notes?

E-mail is not as personal as a handwritten note. If you are following tradition by having a wedding celebration, try to follow tradition by writing your own note by hand. Besides, not everyone has E-mail.

13

FINISHING TOUCHES:

MISCELLANEOUS SERVICES

Garden of Earthly Joy: Flowers

Who pays for the ceremony flowers?

The bride's family pays for flowers that decorate the site as well as flowers for attendants and honored female relatives. The groom's family pays for the bride's bouquet, groom's boutonniere, boutonnieres for male attendants and honored male relatives, and corsages for both mothers. If the bride has a going-away corsage, the groom (or his family) would also pay for that.

Who pays for the flowers that decorate the reception site?

Traditionally, the bride's family covers this bill.

May we use the ceremony flowers at the reception site?

Yes. You will have to assign someone to transport the flowers between the two places and then arrange them at the new location.

Picture Perfect

I want a visual record of our wedding day, but I don't want the photographer to "take over," as happens at so many weddings. How do I keep the photographer from intruding on the celebration?

Tell the photographer about your concerns. Remember, this service provider works for you. There are many ways to take photographs discreetly. If your photographer is a professional, he or she can take lovely and memorable photos and videos with minimal disturbance.

Our family will be together for the first time in years on my wedding day. I wanted to have the photographer take some group family photos between the ceremony and reception. My fiancé is concerned it will take too long. What should we do about photographs between the ceremony and reception? Won't two hours be enough time for our wedding photos and these family photographs?

It depends, but probably not. Today's trend of numerous "photo opportunities" between the ceremony and reception has delayed many receptions, angered guests, and left the newly married couple arriving at their reception exhausted. The purpose of a gap between the two occasions is supposed to provide an opportunity for the bride and groom to rest and relax on a hectic and highly emotional day. You had best use the time that way, too. Perhaps the family photographs can be taken before the ceremony or at a later point in the reception.

How do we notify the guests that we want no flash photos taken at the ceremony?

A sign just outside the entrance saying, "No Flash Photography, Please" should do the trick. If you have programs at your ceremony, you might mention it there as well.

My parents will pay for the photography, so naturally they will receive a set. My fiancé's mother seems to think my parents should also buy them a set. Must the bride's family purchase a set of wedding photographs for the groom's family?

Your family is not required to pay for the family of the groom's pictures. Your family is obligated to notify them when the proofs are available and to give them an opportunity to view the proofs and order their own photographs. However, the groom's family should pay for any pictures that they purchase.

Must we give our wedding attendants group photographs?

Many couples purchase frames and give photographs from the wedding as their attendant's gift. However, you are not required to give any particular item as your gift. What you purchase is your decision.

Production Values: Tips and Gratuities

Why should I tip?

In many service industries, especially among food and beverage providers, employees are paid a very minimum wage. They are expected to make the bulk of their income from tips. The tips are an additional incentive for providing efficient, gracious service.

Who distributes the gratuities?

The best man (or honor attendant) for the groom, the reception host, or the wedding consultant.

Who gets tipped?

Ceremony helpers, such as altar servers and the cantor. Tip anyone who makes an extra effort, such as the organist performing special music. Also tip any service providers, unless the tip is included in their fee.

Do I always have to leave a tip?

No. If the service is bad and it's the service provider's fault, if the gratuity has already been added to your bill, or if the service provider was rude, tipping is not necessary.

What is the percentage rule of thumb?

The fancier the location and occasion, the bigger the compensation. Generally, 15 to 20 percent.

What is an easy way to compute tips?

A 15 percent tip equals 10 percent plus half of that; a 20 percent tip, 10 percent times 2.

Our reception site has washroom attendants and valet parking. We want to pay their tips ourselves so our guests do not have to feel obligated. How do I indicate that all tips have been prepaid?

Display signs stating, "The host has prepaid all gratuities" in appropriate locations.

Who is tipped and how much?

Waitpersons: 15 to 20 percent of the bill.

Banquet Manager: 15 to 20 percent of the food and drink bill. If you pay the banquet manager, he or she distributes the tips among the rest of the staff.

Bartender: 15 to 20 percent of the bill.

Cloakroom attendant: $1.00 per coat, $2.00 if you also checked other items.

Musician: The host tips each musician $10.00 to $20.00; guests tip $1.00 per special request.

Valet parking: $1.00 to $2.00 per car.

14

WHEN
BAD
THINGS
HAPPEN

Expect the Unexpected

I have this horror that somehow my wedding gown will be destroyed before I make it to the altar. I envision spilling coffee on it or tripping and tearing it. Is there anything I can do ahead of time to ensure that this won't happen?

There are no guarantees, but it helps to be prepared. Any bride should make sure that her honor attendant has safety pins, needle, and thread handy throughout the day. When you select your dress, ask what would remove stains on that particular fabric—and keep a bottle of it handy. And if the worst possible thing happens, make the best of it. I know one bride whose dress caught on fire due to her father's carelessly handling a cigarette just before the ceremony. Another bride's three-foot train was caught outside the limousine door and dragged through the muddy streets on the way to the ceremony. And another bride's sister accidentally stepped on her hem causing a huge tear in the front of the dress just before she walked up the aisle. They all survived, are still happily married, and, believe it or not, laugh about it now.

I've been having nightmares about being stood up at the altar. My fiancé assures me he has no plans to abandon me, but I'm so terrified that it will happen I can barely concentrate, much less sleep. Any suggestions?

Everyone has such terrors. Too many movies have shown a bride or groom left standing at the altar before the ceremony. In reality, it doesn't happen that often. If for some reason it does, he will look like a dim-witted, spineless creep. To allow the planning to continue and then, in the most cowardly way imaginable, bail out at the last minute is not only vile, it is immoral. If he's truly that deceitful, then he doesn't deserve you. It would be better for you to endure an hour of embarrassment and lose some deposits than to be legally bound in marriage to such a person. Talk to your fiancé about your fears.

My ex-boyfriend keeps threatening to turn up at the ceremony and make a scene. I'm afraid to tell my fiancé, because I don't want them to confront each other and have a fight. If I tell the ushers to watch for him they will tell my fiancé. I'm terrified that he will ruin my wedding day. What should I do if my ex-boyfriend comes to the ceremony?

Consider having a calm, mutual friend talk to your former boyfriend about his plans. If your ex-boyfriend genuinely intends to attend the ceremony, hire an off-duty police officer as security with instructions to escort him from the scene upon arrival. Despite your fears, you should also talk to your fiancé. It is not good to hide things from each other, and you don't want any part of your wedding to be based on deception. If your fiancé is so hotheaded that you fear what he will do despite your pleas, it may be that he is not emotionally mature enough for marriage.

It's All over But the Crying: The Broken Engagement

If I break off an engagement, may I keep the ring?

No. You should return the ring and all other valuable gifts to your former fiancé.

My fiancé broke off our engagement one week before the wedding. I have all these shower gifts and wedding gifts. May I keep the gifts?

No. You should return all gifts—engagement, shower, and wedding—with a note explaining why.

I hate the thought of writing notes explaining why our engagement was ended. Must I provide a reason?

No. Just mail a simple note to gift givers saying that you are sorry, but the engagement was broken and that the gift they sent you is enclosed.

Should I announce in the newspapers that the engagement is off?

If the invitations have not been sent, a simple notice that your engagement has been broken by mutual agreement can be sent to the newspapers.

It Was a Dark and Stormy Day: The Canceled Wedding

What if something terrible happens and I have to cancel the wedding?

Just as with any other occasion, sometimes a delay or cancellation is necessary. It might be due to death, illness, loss of a job, or the need to reconsider your future together. If the invitations have not been mailed, you need to notify only members of your wedding party, immediate family, close friends, and any service providers whose services you have reserved for that date.

We have to cancel our wedding and the invitations have already been sent. May I notify everyone by mail?

Yes, but only if you are absolutely sure that the guests will receive your notification at least one week before the wedding date.

How would I word such a notice?

It would be issued by the same person that issued the invitations. Here is an example: Mr. and Mrs. Sheldon Huong announce that the marriage of their daughter Amelia Tai to Mr. Lee Ling will not take place.

I have this nightmare that something will happen to cancel the wedding on that day. How can I possibly reach two hundred people if that happens?

At that point, enlist the help of the bridal party to contact everyone by telephone. No one needs to offer a reason, just the information that the event will not take place.

What do I do if my fiancé dies right before the wedding?

In this case, you needn't return gifts or the ring, unless the ring was a family heirloom that his parents would like to have kept in the family. A note or telephone call to the invited guests who may not have heard about the sad incident is also necessary.

What else must I do if I cancel the wedding?

You must return any gifts you have received, including your engagement ring. If your wedding party has paid for their attire, it is polite to reimburse them for that expense, if possible.

15

ADVENTURES IN GOOD FORM:

DO-IT-YOURSELF ETIQUETTE

Mind Your Manners

What is etiquette?

Etiquette is the rules that we all practice in our society and our culture to get along with other people. For the most part, we practice etiquette because we want our lives to run smoothly, without offending people or seeming offensive. Everyday etiquette we practice is personal hygiene, chewing with our mouths closed, or saying "please" and "thank you."

I never worried about etiquette before. Why does it seem to be such a huge part of wedding planning?

How often do you get married? The traditions are unfamiliar because they don't touch our lives in a serious way very often. Yet these customs add distinction to a very important milestone. At a time when you must make many decisions, the guidelines make it easier to understand what has worked for those who have done this before.

Who makes up these rules?

Everybody has made up etiquette by practicing it and deciding if it works well enough to pass on. People who write etiquette books gather and organize the accepted standards. Through experience and research, people learn to apply tradition and customs to new situations. If you are confronted with an unusual situation, ask yourself these three questions: What makes the most sense for everyone? What causes the fewest problems? What reflects our culture's traditions?

Isn't etiquette old-fashioned?

Getting married is an old-fashioned, time-honored tradition. There are many traditions that we follow every day. These show their value to everyone because they have stood the test of time.

We're simple, middle-class people. Isn't etiquette something only rich people should know?

Wealthier people often have extremely formal weddings. And it's true that in the most formal weddings people are expected to carefully follow customary protocols. However, we all try to practice good manners. Etiquette is just a way of spelling out what the proper behavior would be in a particular wedding situation.

I never learned proper table manners. How do I eat in public without embarrassing myself?

Sit up straight, elbows in, and never have more than your hands and wrists on the table. Put your napkin in your lap. If your hands aren't on the table they should be in your lap. Don't cut up all your meal before you start to eat, and avoid taking huge mouthfuls of food. Don't wave your eating utensils while you talk. Chew with your mouth closed. Never fix your hair or apply makeup at the table.

What is the rule about elbows on the table?

Having elbows on the table is never appropriate when you are eating. However, at a large formal dinner or in a noisy dining situation, it is acceptable to put your elbows on the table to help you lean forward to hear or talk to others.

How do I properly use my napkin?

Place it on your lap. When you are finished eating, do not wipe your mouth. Instead, blot it with your napkin. When the meal is finished, do not crumple the napkin, throw it on the plate, or try to refold it. Place it on the left side of your plate in loose folds, or replace it in the napkin ring if those are provided.

Is it true that the guests may not start eating before the bride and groom start?

Yes. Polite guests wait for the bride and groom to begin eating before they begin.

Which silverware do I use?

Start with those farthest from the plate; that is, use the silverware from the outside in. The only exception is if the table has been set incorrectly and it would be impractical to eat with the next available implement.

Where do I place the silverware when I've finished eating?

The knife and fork are placed beside each other on the dinner plate at a diagonal angle, from upper left to lower right. Handles extend about one-half inch over the edge of the plate. Your dessert spoon or fork is placed on that plate or bowl when you are finished. Never leave your spoon inside your coffee cup. Place the spoon on the saucer.

Which foods are acceptable to eat with my fingers?

Bread (in bite-sized pieces), cherry tomatoes (unless served in a salad), chicken and frog legs (except at formal dinners), fresh vegetables (no double dipping), olives, pizza, sandwiches, tacos, and tortillas.

Please settle an argument. Must I leave the table to blow my nose?

No, but you shouldn't use your napkin unless it's an emergency.

Cover your mouth and nose with your handkerchief or tissue, and turn slightly away from the table and other diners.

Controversial Subjects

We moved our wedding date forward two months because the hall we wanted became available. Now everyone assumes that I am pregnant. How do I deal with this?

You cannot really resolve these sort of rumors, no matter how rude and frustrating they are to you both. The proof will be when no baby is born on the predicted date.

I will be visibly pregnant at our wedding. Should I tell people beforehand?

I would let the word out ahead of time. You really don't want that buzz of surprise following you up the aisle—do you?

We're not even married yet and people want to know when we're having children. What do I tell them?

It is amazing how many people feel perfectly comfortable inquiring about changes in your marital status and reproductive plans. Neither subject is anyone else's business, unless you decide to make it so. "We prefer not to discuss it right now" is the best answer to those inquiries.

My fiancé is black; I am white. I'm afraid that some of my family members will be rude at the wedding to him or his family. What can I do?

You can hope that your family is well mannered enough not to spoil your happiness and that if they genuinely disapprove, they will stay home rather than ruin the celebration. If you don't think your family will behave decently, you might ask a levelheaded mutual friend or relative to talk to them about your concerns. Every family of every race, color, and creed has an occasional ill-mannered lout. Your fiancé's family will hopefully understand this if the worst happens.

I am black; my fiancé is white. His family is very patronizing. What can I do?

Ignore it as best you can. Hopefully, as your fiancé's family gets to know you better and appreciates your good qualities, they will relate to you as an individual person, not as a representative of an entire race.

I'm marrying a significantly older man. In fact, he has a daughter my age. I have already heard enough crude jokes for a lifetime. In addition, his children are very uncomfortable around me. What can I do?

As far as the crude jokes go, ignore them. Probably, the people who tell them are encouraged when you are upset by them.

You are stepping into a nontraditional place in his children's lives, and they probably don't know how to treat you. You are not their mother, friend, or sibling. You are going to be their dad's wife. It must make them feel a little odd for their dad's wife to be of their generation. Give them time. As they get to know you as a person who loves and cares for their father, they will learn to value you and relate to you in your own right.

My mother has asked me to be maid of honor for her as she marries a man of whom I don't approve. I don't want to hurt her feelings by declining, but I don't want to be any part of this travesty. Any suggestions?

If you disapprove and show it throughout the festivities, it will certainly hurt your mother's feelings more than your declining the role of honor attendant.

My sister is a lesbian and wants to "come out" at our wedding. I feel like it will ruin my wedding day because all of the focus will be on her situation. Am I right to object?

Yes, you are right. Your sister may be thinking it would be a handy time, with all the family gathered all in one place. However, the day that you are pledging to join your life with someone else's should not be disrupted by your sister's announcement of her sexual orientation. I would encourage her very strongly to break the ice beforehand rather than at your wedding. She can begin by informing immediate family members and let the grapevine do the rest.

A Final Note

No matter how hard I have tried, I will have missed some questions that may arise in your particular circumstances. Every family has a variety of situations, customs, and traditions. You and your fiancé both will have your own ideas and predicaments. When you are confronted with a difficult obstacle or problematic person, you need to learn to recognize the heart of the problem. Then, you can find the best solution for your personal needs. Here are a few questions to ask.

What is the real problem? Is the objection based on a genuine or perceived need? Is the person trying to make a statement or is he or she just misinformed about what traditions, customs, and good manners would apply in this situation?

What is that person trying to accomplish? Is the person trying to feel important or superior? Is she concerned about someone else's feelings? Is he trying to get your attention? Is she attempting to control the situation? Knowing people's motivations will help you find a solution and assist them in understanding your decision.

What are you trying to accomplish? You are trying to have a smooth, decorous, trouble-free day. Follow conventional standards and attempt to make as many people as possible happy, including yourself.

What solution has been found in past customs and traditions in somewhat similar circumstances? Because society and its practices are constantly evolving, so are the standards of etiquette. However, if, for example, your problem has to do with ceremony seating, study that section for a general knowledge of how people are seated. That should give you a basis for adaptation and compromise.

What kind of wedding are you having? The more traditional style of wedding you are having, the closer it should adhere to customary protocol. A very formal wedding would follow established procedures. An informal wedding may be quite flexible.

What would a reasonable and unbiased person do in these

circumstances? Be compassionate and empathetic.

Having wisdom is being able to find a fair solution and then apply it with consideration and grace.

Will your decision genuinely harm someone or your relationship with that person? Weigh all possible outcomes. Examine your own motives and use sound judgement. Can you tactfully explain your conclusion in a way the other person can understand? Would you be comfortable being treated the same way in similar circumstances?

Many solutions are just basic common sense.

Here's an example. You are planning to marry outdoors, near the North Carolina coast, during the rainy season. Your mother insists that you should not have a tent because your wedding is too formal. Common sense tells you that you need a place to shield you from possible inclement weather.

Here's another example. Your future mother-in-law objects to the marriage and plans to wear black as a statement of protest. Common sense tells you that the more of an issue you make of this, the more attention she will receive. If you don't tell anyone why she is wearing black, some of your guests will probably just think that she chose that shade of clothing for its known slimming effect.

Our society has evolved to a point where we are all fairly open-minded about propriety and formality. In my family alone, a few generations back a wedding was boycotted by both sides because a Polish man married an Italian woman. In my grandparents' generation, the family was in an uproar and many stayed home when a Catholic man married a Protestant woman. Today we joyously celebrate marriages between all nationalities, faiths, and races. Well, most of us do.

Good manners are a combination of common sense, tradition, and the desire not to offend others. Etiquette is just a road map, and there are often many routes leading to the same successful destination.

Good luck and bon voyage!

Wedding-Speak to English Glossary

Aisle Carpet   Covers the aisle for the processional and recessional at the ceremony site. It is meant to protect long gowns and bridal trains from any dirt carried in by arriving guests.

Announcement   A communication notifying a general group of people. An engagement is usually announced through the newspapers. A marriage is announced through newspapers and sometimes through formally printed or engraved stationery. Announcements are mailed to people you wish to inform who were not invited to the wedding. Announcements are sent after the wedding takes place.

Ascot   Neck scarf often worn in place of a bow tie. It is tied with the broad ends laid flat. Sometimes they come pre-tied. An ascot is usually worn with a stickpin.

Attendants   Also known as members of the wedding party—the bridesmaids, groomsmen, ushers, flower girl, and ring bearer.

Attire   Clothing in wedding-speak.

Best Man   Groom's honor attendant. He or she has many specific duties and obligations.

Blusher Veil   Veil worn over the bride's face in the processional. During the ceremony it is moved back over the bride's head.

Bouquet   Collection of flowers gathered together at the stems, usually accented with lace and ribbons.

Boutonniere   Flower or several flowers worn by males in their buttonholes.

Bow Tie   Made of formal fabric and tied in a bow. Worn with a tuxedo or dinner jacket.

Breakfast Reception   Takes place between 10 A.M. and 12 P.M. Usually a simple breakfast with cake as dessert.

Buffet   Dining arrangement where food is congregated in one location and the guests serve themselves. In most weddings, seating and tables are provided. In less formal settings, the guests dine holding their plates.

Cake Topper   Figurines or flowers set on top of the wedding cake.

Cantor   This person chants prayers and responses in some religious ceremonies.

Cash Bar   Misguided practice initiated by cash-strapped couples who want to serve alcohol at their wedding. If you can't afford to pay for it, don't serve it.

Ceremony   Portion of the day when the bride and groom exchange vows and actually get married.

Cocktail Reception   Takes place between 4 and 6 P.M. Beverages, hors d'oeuvres, and cake.

Corsage   Small bouquet of flowers worn by women on the wrist, waist, or shoulder.

Cummerbund   Sash worn as a belt, it covers the pant button, top of the zipper, and where the shirt tucks into the pants.

Cutaway   Formal daytime equivalent of a tailcoat. At the waist, the front tapers gently to the back in a tail.

Denomination   Particular sect of a religious creed. In Christianity, for example, there are Baptists, Lutherans, Presbyterians, Methodists, Catholics, and many others.

Dinner Jacket   Coat traditionally used in semiformal weddings. Also known as a tuxedo jacket.

Dinner Reception   Traditional celebration beginning between 6 and 8 P.M. with dinner and music.

Engagement   When you promise to marry each other, you become engaged.

Evening Ceremony   Takes place after 6 P.M. More formal than daytime.

Fiancé   Term the female uses for the male she is engaged to marry.

Fiancée   Term the male uses for the female he is engaged to marry.

Flower Girl   Young girl under the age of ten who walks in the processional. Traditionally she sprinkled flowers or flower petals in the bride's path. Many ceremony sites no longer permit this. In those locations she carries a basket of flowers and looks cute.

Formal Ceremony   The larger, more lavish, and elaborate kind of celebration.

Four-in-hand   Standard necktie, tied in a slipknot.

French Cuff   Band at the bottom of a shirtsleeve held together by a stud or cuff link instead of buttons.

Garter   Elastic covered with satin, ruffles, or feathers worn above the bride's knee.

Gratuity   Another word for tip. A bonus given for a service provided.

Groomsmen   Men in the wedding party. In formal, traditional weddings they do not usher. Their primary role is escorting bridesmaids.

Guest Book   Blank book that is placed on a stand at the reception. Each guest is invited to sign their name.

Head Table   Table where the bride, groom, and their entire wedding party are seated.

Head Usher   Coordinates the seating arrangements at the ceremony, usually designated by the groom.

Honor Attendant   Role of the best man or maid/matron of honor. Sometimes, when the best man is a woman or the maid/matron of honor is a man, then they are simply referred to as honor attendants.

Honor Table   Special table for seating particular guests. If the parents of the bride and groom do not sit at the head table, they would sit here. This table might also include grandparents, godparents, siblings, the ceremony officiant, and any distinguished guests (such as the mayor or a famous rock star). There can be more than one honor table, but it is best to intermix the families.

Host   Male sponsor of the entertainment and/or celebration. At a wedding this person is traditionally the bride's father.

Hostess   Female sponsor of the entertainment and/or celebration. At a wedding this person is traditionally the bride's mother.

In-law   Term used to define relationships created by marriage. Your spouse's mother becomes your mother-in-law.

In the ribbons   Reserved seating at the ceremony site set near the front for very close family members and extremely important guests.

Informal Wedding   Simplest style of ceremony, such as only the bride and groom at a justice of the peace.

Junior Bridesmaid   Young female attendant, in the ages of ten to fourteen years. She can dress identically or differently from the other attendants and does not require a groomsman to escort her in the recessional or throughout the day.

Long Jacket   Formalwear coat that reaches mid-thigh length.

Luncheon Reception   Takes place between 12 and 2 P.M. Usually includes meal, beverages, and cake.

Maid of Honor   Bride's honor attendant who has never married.

Matron of Honor   Bride's honor attendant who has already been or is currently married.

Officiant   The person who performs the wedding ceremony.

Out-of-town guest   Someone who has traveled some distance to attend your festivities. The rule of thumb is more than a four-hour drive or more than one-hundred sixty miles away.

Personal Shower   Intimate gathering for the bride. Gifts include lingerie and other sensitive private items.

Place Cards   Cards with the guest's name printed or handwritten on the front. The card is put at the place setting where the guest is to be seated during the dinner.

Pocket Square   Creative name for the small handkerchief of linen or silk that peaks out of the breast pocket of the man's jacket. It is worn in place of boutonnieres.

Pouf Veil   Small gathered tuft of veiling that is attached to the back of the headpiece.

Processional   The walk the wedding party takes up the aisle before the ceremony.

Programs   Bulletins that provide information helpful to the guests. Information might include the names of the wedding party; special songs and prayers to be performed; and guidelines to following the service for those who might be unfamiliar with the particular ritual.

Receiving line Line formed by the primary members of the wedding party to greet guests either after the ceremony or before the reception.

Reception Celebration gathering that takes place after the wedding ceremony.

Recessional Return walk made down the aisle by the wedding party after the ceremony. It is in reverse order of the processional. The bride and groom lead the recessional.

Rehearsal Practice for the wedding ceremony, primarily of the processional and recessional. Traditionally takes place the night before the wedding.

Rehearsal Dinner Traditional dinner the night before the wedding hosted by the groom's family. Guests include the entire wedding party, all parents, grandparents, siblings, and special guests who have arrived from out of town.

Response card Controversial (etiquette-wise) card included with wedding invitations, usually with a self-addressed stamped envelope. The purpose of the card is to make it easy for guests to tell you if they will attend your celebration.

Ring Bearer Traditionally, a boy under eight years of age who marches in the processional carrying the wedding rings to the altar.

Ring Bearer's Pillow Small lace or satin pillow that's carried up the aisle by a young boy. The wedding rings are tied to the pillow.

Semiformal Somewhere between formal and informal.

Shower Party whose purpose is to "rain" gifts upon the guest(s) of honor.

Stroller Jacket Also called a "walking coat." The cut is slightly longer than a suit jacket. Usually worn in black or gray before 6 P.M. at semi-formal weddings.

Studs Small fasteners (a knob and disk connected by a stem) used in place of buttons on very formal clothing. They are often gold or have gemstones in gold settings.

Tailcoat   Long formal coat completely cutaway at the front waist. The back is very long and tapered.

Tea Reception   Held between 2 and 5 P.M. Traditionally the food is cake, punch, and coffee.

Toast   Custom of communally drinking to a person or an idea. One person announces the purpose and the others raise their glass, and drink "to it". The only exception would be the person being toasted. They smile and nod.

Train   Material that extends along the ground behind the bride's dress. Varies from one to ten feet in length.

Trousseau   Clothing, linens, and other articles the bride has accumulated prior to marriage, specifically for use during her married life.

Tuxedo   Catchall word in formalwear. Originally, a tuxedo described the jacket worn for a formal wedding after 6 P.M. Now it might mean any semiformal coat or the entire formalwear ensemble.

Usher   Male attendant who seats guests at the ceremony.

Valet Parking   Vehicles are parked and retrieved for the guests by workers hired specifically for that purpose.

Waistcoat   Distinctive term for vests worn with formalwear.

Waltz Veil   Ankle-length veil.

Wedding Party   Bride, groom, both sets of their parents, and the male and female attendants.

White Tie   Most formal men's style of attire. You wear a black coat with tails, matching trousers, winged-collar shirt, and a white tie and vest.

Winged Collar   Shirt collar has folds at the front center, with a tiny v-wing shape on each side. Usually worn with a thinner tie.

Other wedding titles available from Chicago Review Press:

THE BRIDE'S THANK YOU GUIDE
Thank-You Writing Made Easy
94 pages, $5.95
ISBN: 1-55652-200-2

THE BRIDE'S MONEY BOOK
How to Have a Champagne Wedding on a Ginger-Ale Budget
98 pages, $11.95
ISBN: 1-55652-261-4

THE BRIDE TO BRIDE BOOK
A Complete Wedding Planner for the Bride
150 pages, $11.95
ISBN: 1-55652-270-3